MILLIONS OF AMERICANS SUFFER FROM ANXIETY OR DEPRESSION. PHYSICAL HEALTH, JOB PERFORMANCE, PERSONAL RELATIONSHIPS ARE ALL ADVERSELY AFFECTED. NOW, THANKS TO SAFER MEDICATION AND INCREASINGLY SOPHISTICATED THERAPY, ALL FORMS OF ANXIETY OR DEPRESSION CAN BE TREATED QUICKLY, AND WITH LASTING RESULTS.

The Pill Book of Anxiety and Depression, written especially for the consumer, tells you everything you need to know about the medications used in the treatment of these illnesses. Here is all the information right at your fingertips, including cautions and warnings, side effects, adverse reactions, usual dosage levels, and the potential for overdose. Plus, the different kinds and causes of anxiety and depression, and how to overcome them for a more productive work life and more fulfilling personal life.

The purpose of this book is to provide educational information to the public concerning the drugs most commonly prescribed by doctors for the treatment of anxiety and depression. It is not intended to be complete or exhaustive or in any respect a substitute for personal medical care. *Only a doctor may prescribe these drugs and the exact dosages that should be taken.*

While every effort has been made to reproduce products on the cover and insert of this book in an exact fashion, certain variations of size or color may be expected as a result of the photographic process. Furthermore, pictures identified as brand-name drugs should not be confused with their generic counterparts, and vice versa. *In any event, the reader should not rely on the photographic image to identify any pills depicted herein, but should rely soley on the doctor's description as dispensed by the pharmacist.*

THE PILL BOOK OF ANXIETY & DEPRESSION

BERT STERN

Producer

LAWRENCE D. CHILNICK

Editor-In-Chief

TEXT BY

R. C. Garrett

U. G. Waldmeyer

MEDICAL CONSULTANT

Alan F. Schatzberg, M.D.
Associate Professor of Psychiatry,
Harvard Medical School

PRODUCTION

Daniel Montopoli

BANTAM BOOKS
TORONTO • NEW YORK • LONDON • SYDNEY • AUCKLAND

Special thanks to Jeff Packer
and Dave Phillips, Carlyle Chemists,
New York City

THE PILL BOOK OF ANXIETY AND DEPRESSION
A Bantam Book / January 1986

ISBN 0-553-25417-0

Published simultaneously in the United States and Canada

Bantam Books are published by Bantam Books, Inc. Its trademark, consisting of the words ''Bantam Books'' and the portrayal of a rooster, is Registered in U.S. Patent and Trademark Office and in other countries. Marca Registrada. Bantam Books, Inc., 666 Fifth Avenue, New York, New York 10103.

PRINTED IN THE UNITED STATES OF AMERICA

O   0 9 8 7 6 5 4 3 2 1

Contents

How to Use This Book   1

I. Anxiety and Depression in the 1980s   7

   1. Two Separate Illnesses   9
   2. Anxiety—What It Is . . . and Isn't   12
      How Anxiety Affects Body And Mind
   3. Phobias and Panic Attacks   19
   4. Causes of Anxiety   24
   5. Treating Anxiety   28
   6. Depression—What Is It?   34
      Are You Depressed?
   7. The Many Faces of Depression   42
      How Depression Affects Body and Mind
   8. Causes of Depression   47
   9. Help and Treatment for Depression   59

II. The Most Commonly Prescribed Anxiety and
    Depression Drugs in the United States, Ge-
    neric and Brand Names, with Complete De-
    scriptions of Drugs and Their Effects   69

1. General Information About Drug Types   71
2. Drug Profiles   80

III. Color Plates

Pill Identification Charts

Appendices

A—Phobias   178
B—Some Physical Illnesses that
   Can Cause Anxiety   180
C—Some Drugs That Can Cause
   Anxiety   182
D—Some Physical Illnesses That Can
   Cause Depression   184
E—Some Drugs That Can Cause
   Depression   186
   Sources   191
   Index of Generic and Brand Name Drugs   196

HOW TO USE THIS BOOK

The Pill Book of Anxiety and Depression is divided into three main sections:

1. Information about the many aspects of anxiety and depression, including details about their nature, treatments, and facts you should know about living with both illnesses.

2. Easy-to-read profiles of the drugs most often prescribed to treat anxiety and depression.

3. Life-sized pictures of the anxiety and depression drugs most commonly prescribed in the United States.

The photo system for checking medications in *The Pill Book of Anxiety and Depression* is designed to help you quickly identify the drug you're about to take. Included are the most popular brand-name drugs, and many of the drugs most frequently prescribed by generic name. Although several dosage levels may be included, other dosage levels may be omitted because they are prescribed less often.

The drugs are organized alphabetically and have been reproduced as faithfully as possible. While every effort has been made to depict the drugs accurately, certain variations in size and color must be expected as a result of the photographic and printing processes. Therefore, you should never rely solely on the photographic image to identify any pill, but should check with your doctor or pharmacist if you have any questions whatsoever about the identification.

Most, but not all, of the drugs in the color section can be matched with your anxiety or depression medication by matching your pill with the following on each photo:

   • The imprinted company logo (i.e., "Lilly," "Roche")
   • The product strength (i.e., "250 mg.," "10 mg.")
   • The product code number, which may be imprinted on the pill

Because many generic drugs look the same as their brand-name counterparts, some manufacturers have started printing the product name on each pill.

To find out more about the drug shown, check the descriptive text on the pages referred to in the photo caption. The pill profiles provide complete descriptions of the most often prescribed generic and brand-name anxiety and depression drugs. The descriptions give you detailed information about your prescriptions. The easy-to-read profiles are listed alphabetically by their generic names (except when the product profiled is a combination of two or more generic drugs, in which case the popular brand names for these combinations are profiled in alphabetical order).

The drug profiles contain the following information:

Generic Name: The generic name is the drug's

common name, or chemical name, as approved by the Food and Drug Administration (FDA).

Brand Name(s): The brand name is the name given by a particular drug company to identify its product. For example, Valium is a brand name for the generic drug diazepam. When particular drugs are also sold under their generic names, that information is given here.

Ingredients: The ingredients are listed whenever an anxiety or depression medication is a combination of two or more generic drugs. In this case, the drug will be listed alphabetically under its brand name, rather than the name of one of its ingredients.

Type of Drug: How the individual drug is classified, which may indicate its relation to other drugs. For example, Antipress, classed as a tricyclic antidepressant, is closely related to other antidepressants like Norpramin, Adapin, and Endep. More information on these drug types is provided at the beginning of section II.

Prescribed for: The condition(s) for which a drug is most often prescribed. In some instances, a drug listed in this book may be prescribed for conditions other than anxiety and depression. If you are unsure why you were told to take one of these medications, ask your doctor.

Cautions and Warnings: Any drug can be harmful if you are sensitive to any of its actions. The information provided here alerts you to possible allergic reactions, and to certain personal physical conditions, such as pregnancy and thyroid disease, which should be taken into consideration if the drug is prescribed for you. A general note of caution regarding anxiety and depression drugs: children sometimes respond differently from adults if given some of the drugs described in this book. A drug that brings calm to an adult may make some children irritable or hyperactive. Anxiety and depression drugs should be given to children only after careful evaluation by a doctor experienced in treating children, and only when the potential benefits clearly outweigh the possible adverse effects.

Possible Side Effects: These are the more common side effects to be expected from the drug.

Possible Adverse Effects: Less common effects of a pill that may be cause for concern. If you are not sure whether you are experiencing an adverse reaction, ALWAYS CALL YOUR DOCTOR.

Drug Interactions: This section tells you which other drugs should be avoided when taking a particular anxiety or depression medication. Drug interactions with other pills, alcohol, food, or other substances can cause death. Interactions are more common than overdoses. It is very important to be careful when drinking alcohol with any medication, or when taking several drugs at the same time. Be sure to inform your doctor of any medication—prescription or nonprescription—you have been taking. Your pharmacist should also keep a record of all your prescription and over-the-counter drugs. This listing, generally called a Patient Drug Profile, is used to review your record should problems arise. You may want to keep your own drug record and bring it to your pharmacist for review whenever a new medicine is added.

Usual Dose: The maximum and minimum amounts of a drug that are usually prescribed. However, you may be given different dosage instructions by your doctor. It is important to check with your doctor if you are confused about how often to take a pill, and when, or if you have been given a dosage different from that indicated in this book. You should not change the prescribed dosage of any drug you are taking without first talking with your doctor.

Overdose: Symptoms of a drug overdose and the immediate steps you should take if an overdose occurs are detailed whenever there is a danger of an overdose reaction.

If you read something in *The Pill Book of Anxiety and Depression* that does not coincide with your doctor's instructions, call your doctor. He or she may have had special reasons for prescribing different medications or different dosages from those referred to here.

Any drug can have serious side effects if used improperly or abused. We advise you to learn all you can about the drugs you're taking—the benefits and dangers alike.

I
Anxiety and Depression
in the 1980s

1.

TWO SEPARATE ILLNESSES

Anxiety. Depression. Sometimes they are so similar that even doctors have trouble telling them apart.

Prolonged anxiety can result in depression. Depression, on the other hand, can exaggerate or even trigger anxiety attacks.

Yet, despite the close relationships between anxiety and depression, they are very different illnesses, each capable in its own way of destroying families, wrecking careers, and ruining health.

Almost everybody occasionally experiences some degree of anxiety—and even a period of depression—as a normal response to the stresses of everyday life. Such episodes are seldom cause for concern, and usually pass quickly without the need for drugs or professional care.

But anxiety and depression can also devastate. You may know someone who is afraid of heights—who turns pale and perspires heavily if required to visit an apartment or office in a tall building. One of your friends might be terrified of leaving home, whether to go shopping or to see a movie. Such fears, or "phobias," are a common form of anxiety.

Depression, too, can critically alter the lives of its victims and their families. Even a mild depression may cause insomnia, sap enthusiasm, affect job performance, or strain relationships.

However, anxiety and depression need no longer be as feared as they were until a few years ago. Today, these illnesses can generally be treated successfully with the medications and therapies described in this book. It is indeed a particularly difficult case of anxiety—or a severe form of depression— that does not respond to modern medicine.

TRADITIONAL VS. MODERN VIEW OF ANXIETY AND DEPRESSION

Traditional

Anxiety and depression are mental illnesses

Modern
There are many causes:

- *DIET. Certain foods can cause either anxiety or depression in some people*

- *DRUGS. Some drugs, including frequently prescribed ones, can cause or contribute to anxiety and/or depression*

- *ACCIDENTS. Physical injury can bring on episodes of either illness*

- *HEREDITY. Your biological makeup can predispose you to anxiety or depression*

Traumatic events can cause anxiety and depression. So can the tensions of daily life. Most people, however, are able to handle these crises without long-lasting ill effects.

In addition to personal experiences, diet can change a person's reasonable concern about, say, flying in an airplane, into a deep, incapacitating anxiety over flying. Studies demonstrate, too, that many drugs can turn an ordinary case of "the blues" into a serious depression.

Learning as much as possible about anxiety and depression can help you recognize when to seek professional help either for someone you love or for yourself. *The Pill Book of Anxiety and Depression* tries to provide the information you need to better understand these illnesses, as well as how doctors across the country are most likely to treat them.

2.

ANXIETY—WHAT IT IS ...
AND ISN'T

- *Anxiety can be a completely normal reaction, or a totally inappropriate response*
- *There are subconscious ways in which most people deal with anxiety*
- *Anxiety, phobias, and panic attacks are interlinked*
- *Anxiety is not the same as fear*

You may already have a good notion about what anxiety is—and isn't—from your own experience, and how it differs from fear.

Both anxiety and fear can be beneficial warning signs of potential danger. They put us on notice that something dangerous—even something we cannot yet identify—may require us either to fight or to plan our escape. They help prepare us for "fight or flight" by setting off a complex system of physical responses that allows us to run faster, scream louder, or fight harder. Fear and anxiety can help us mobilize for survival.

Fear is a response to a *specific danger*, one you can see, hear, taste, or feel. It's what you might experience if confronted by a gun-wielding mugger or trapped in a burning building. Fear is a reaction to an obvious and real threat.

Then there are feelings of uneasiness, apprehension, tension, and dread that most people experience at one time or another. These may be related to specific events such as a new job, an exam, an illness, moving to a new city, or to broad social problems such as poverty or the state of the economy.

When such feelings are caused by anticipation of danger, *when it is unclear whether real danger exists,* they are called anxiety. Anxiety is a reaction to vague, diffuse, and sometimes imaginary dangers.

Anxiety is most often based on a valid, rational understanding of the world in which we live, and is frequently a normal reaction to stress. During an era of worsening global relationships, who wouldn't feel anxious about the possibility of war? Beginning a new job, who wouldn't be concerned about the future?

Actually, anxiety frequently serves a useful purpose. Stage fright—known also as "performance anxiety"—can help a person speak well before an audience by forcing him or her to pay close attention to pronunciation and posture.

Sometimes, however, anxiety is clearly unrealistic or irrational. Stage fright can become so overwhelming that it prevents a person from speaking even in front of family members or close friends.

Some people call anxiety the "what if . . ." illness: "What if I say something silly and embarrass myself?"

"What if the airplane I'm on crashes?"

"What if I open the closet and a rat jumps out?"

"What if something dreadful happens the moment I turn off the lights?"

An anxiety victim may be well aware that nothing terrible is likely to happen just because the lights are turned off. Yet he or she can still be plagued by a barrage of "what if . . ." questions that can turn harmless darkness into a seemingly overwhelming danger.

Intense anxiety about speaking, heights, rodents, or darkness is seldom the appropriate response to the real dangers these things may pose, unless, of course, they do represent some kind of immediate hazard.

Yet, such deep anxieties are an everyday part of many people's lives. Their anxieties can cause them severe emotional discomfort, serious family problems, professional hardships, and even physical illness.

Everyone sooner or later feels some degree of anxiety, yet most of us remain relatively untroubled by it. Without realizing it, the majority of people have found ways to deal with what, for others, is a crippling illness.

Adaptive behavior is a common technique used subconsciously to divert anxiety into less-harmful directions. Spending money, doing something useful but not essential (scrubbing the floor, polishing the car), developing a sense of humor, working harder, or rewarding yourself with a special snack are some examples. All these are also termed coping behaviors.

Then there are so-called defense mechanisms. These are largely subconscious and vary widely but serve the same basic function: to alter the way reality is perceived, so that anxiety is no longer felt so strongly.

Among the most common mental defenses described by researchers:

• *Conversion.* Anxiety is transformed into physical symptoms, such as headaches or upset stomachs.

• *Suppression.* The cause of anxiety is put out of mind—in effect, ignored—either deliberately or subconsciously.

• *Repression.* Forgetfulness takes place at times of severe anxiety.

• *Denial.* The existence of unpleasant realities is not admitted. This is an automatic process.

Some methods of dealing with anxiety can themselves threaten health. If anxiety is "converted" to an upset stomach, for instance, the stomach problem itself can become an unpleasant illness. Similarly, using alcohol or drugs to ease anxiety can be extremely harmful.

One form of conversion is the "anxiety heart attack," which mimics all the symptoms of a real heart attack, and can even threaten life, but doesn't involve the heart muscle at all. Clearly, it is better to overcome anxiety than to "convert" it.

When these mental mechanisms fail to ease the anxiety, it can blossom into either a phobia or a panic attack. Both phobias and panic attacks are discussed in detail in chapter 3.

The Many Faces of Anxiety

Two very common forms of anxiety are often labeled as "separation anxiety" and "castration anxiety." Separation anxiety is considered normal among children, who are deeply dependent on their parents for every aspect of life and are frightened when separated from them until they grow accustomed to new surroundings, such as school.

HOW ANXIETY AFFECTS BODY AND MIND

When we suppress anxiety, consciously or subconsciously, our bodies and minds often find ways to express it. Among them:

Physical Symptoms

Dizziness
Sweating
Faintness
Weakness
Tension headache
Fatigue
Nausea
Dry mouth
Abdominal pain
Cramps
Diarrhea
Pounding heartbeat
Chest pain or tightness
Anorexia (no appetite)
Difficulty in breathing
Difficulty in swallowing
Muscle tension
Sexual disturbances

Emotional/Psychological Symptoms

Nervousness
Feeling of isolation
Irritability
Frantic behavior

Among adults, separation anxiety may be expressed as the constant need to be loved, approved, and accepted. Without this continuous reassurance, the anxiety victim feels insecure and frightened.

Castration anxiety involves the need to succeed. In a competitive society where status is threatened by the possibility of job loss, not getting a promotion, or not being recognized as a contributing member of a group (whether family or company), anxiety can soon become overwhelming.

There are many other forms of anxiety. In fact, the word *anxiety* is the catch-all name for many illnesses, each with a different cause and different symptoms. All, however, are related to an underlying feeling of potential doom.

Some of anxiety's many other faces:

• *Phobias.* Powerful, illogical fears of specific objects or situations (snakes, heights, speaking in public).

• *Generalized anxiety (also called free-floating anxiety).* An overall feeling of anxiety not related to any single specific cause.

• *Panic attacks.* Unpredictable attacks of highly intensified anxiety; the sudden, inappropriate mobilization of the body's defense alarm system.

• *Existential anxiety.* An exaggerated concern with health and the frailty of life (cancer, heart disease, nuclear war).

• *Situational anxiety.* A specific situation (a visit to the doctor to hear results of medical tests; to the boss to learn whether a promotion came through) produces high anxiety.

• *Posttraumatic anxiety.* Stress following a traumatic event (a severe accident, rape, mugging).

• *Obsessive-compulsive anxiety.* Thoughts, for instance, of violence or contamination, become a persistent, irresistible obsession; often joined by an overpowering impulse to perform an irrational act. Victims become anxious when they cannot complete specific compulsive rituals (such as washing their hands several dozen times a day). This pervasive anxiety stems from an underlying phobia, such as a fear of germs, which has begun to dominate the victim's life.

3.

PHOBIAS AND PANIC ATTACKS

- *Phobias strike millions of Americans*
- *Agoraphobia is often accompanied by panic attacks*
- *Panic attacks overwhelm both physically and emotionally*

Phobias are sometimes considered the "diseases of the decade." As many as 20 million Americans suffer from one or more of the many recognized phobias. They are the most frequently discussed—and studied—group of anxieties. The word *phobia* stems from the Greek word *phobe*, meaning "fear."

Phobias are fears (1) that are out of proportion to the circumstances; (2) that cannot be dealt with by reasoning or overcome by willpower; and (3) that result in the victim's avoidance of the feared situation. A phobic person faces even more than the object of the phobia itself; he or she may also be frightened of the very fact that the phobia exists.

Many of us have one or more severe anxieties or even phobias, but usually we deal with them reasonably well simply by avoiding the situations that make us anxious.

Someone afraid of heights, for example, very often can stay away from tall buildings. A person fearful of snakes can avoid outdoor areas where snakes are abundant.

But when a job seeker's only employment possibilities are on high floors of tall buildings, and his or her fear of heights is overwhelming, permanent unemployment may result. Many men and women have had to change careers because they were unreasonably afraid of air travel but their jobs required cross-country or international trips.

It is estimated that one of every nine American adults harbors some kind of "limiting" phobia—that is, a fear that limits his or her activities. This makes phobia the nation's second-largest mental health problem, right after alcoholism. In many instances, phobia and alcoholism may be linked since phobias can increase a person's alcohol consumption.

Research is unveiling more information about the causes of phobias. Gone is the notion that they are imagined fears, which can be controlled merely by willpower. And with the increased knowledge, the treatments for phobias are becoming more effective.

Some phobias are much more common than others. Some strike women more often than men; others, men more frequently than women. While it is widely accepted that women suffer from phobias more than men, this assessment may be partly due to the fact that more women than men consult doctors, and that phobias—and other illnesses—are therefore more frequently diagnosed in women.

Agoraphobia—the fear of open places—attacks

one adult in twenty. Most of its confirmed victims are women, but there is now some evidence that many more men than was previously suspected have the illness. It is possible that male agoraphobics are more successful than women at disguising the disorder.

Agoraphobia victims are afraid of situations that might keep them from returning home quickly, e.g., visiting malls, supermarkets, etc. Many victims are fearful of leaving home at all. In one well-known case, a woman spent decades in or near her house, prior to treatment. Then, after only a few months of treatment, she began visiting stores and theaters regularly.

Agoraphobia is thought to begin with some less-serious form of anxiety, or with panic attacks.

Panic attacks almost always occur suddenly, spontaneously, and erratically, in no specific pattern or situation, particularly among agoraphobics. The attacks can last as long as twenty minutes, during which the heartbeat speeds up, breathing may be

---

PANIC ATTACKS

You may be experiencing a panic attack related to agoraphobia if:

• *You suddenly feel threatened by something you cannot specifically identify*

• *You have trouble breathing, your heartbeat is rapid or erratic, and you break out sweating*

• *You feel overwhelmed by feelings of doom*

• *You need to rush home, or to some other safe place, immediately, regardless of what you're doing.*

SOME COMMON PHOBIAS

Acrophobia—fear of heights
Aerophobia—fear of flying
Agoraphobia—fear of open places
Ailurophobia—fear of cats
Anthropophobia—fear of people
Bathophobia—fear of depth
Claustrophobia—fear of closed spaces
Hematophobia—fear of blood
Iatrophobia—fear of doctors
Monophobia—fear of being alone
Nyctophobia—fear of night
Pathophobia—fear of disease

(A list of additional phobias appears in appendix A.)

---

difficult, and the victim may experience nausea, lightheadedness, and generalized sweating.

The urge to flee or to scream is a common symptom of panic attacks. It is frequently joined by an overwhelming feeling of unreality, impending doom, and "going to pieces."

Victims of panic attacks often retreat to their homes where, they find, the attack quickly subsides. They soon learn to recognize home as their one safe haven. Thus, agoraphobia is as much an intense desire for safety as it is a fear of places away from home. Since victims cannot know where or when a panic attack might take place, they often stay at home to avoid the possibility that one may occur *anywhere.*

GROUPS THAT OFFER HELP FOR ANXIETY AND PHOBIA VICTIMS

If anxiety sometimes overwhelms you, you aren't alone. Some 13 million Americans suffer from various degrees of anxiety, including phobias, panic disorders, and obsessive-compulsive behavior.

Self-help groups—for people with problems like yours—exist around the country. They are often effective in helping people cope with specific types of anxiety, such as fear of airplanes, water, or bridges.

CHAANGE
Center for Help for Agoraphobia/Anxiety
2915 Providence Road
Charlotte, NC 28211
(704) 365-0140
For information on their services, and for audio cassette program, write or call.

Phobia Society of America
5820 Hubbard Drive
Rockville, MD 20852
(301) 231-9350
For information about treatment centers across the country, write or call.

PASS (Panic Attack Sufferer's Support Group)
1042 East 105th St.
Brooklyn, NY 11236
(718) 763-0190
Offers seven-step drug-free program; information given by phone. Trained counselors are recovered agoraphobics.

4.

CASES OF ANXIETY

- *Physical illness may cause anxiety*
- *Drugs or diet can be responsible*
- *Personality also plays a role*

Although we all experience anxiety in one form or another—sometimes beneficial, sometimes destructive—there is clearly a threshold beyond which anxiety requires medical treatment.

When anxiety dominates your life, disrupts your family or other relationships, seriously interferes with your job, or makes it impossible for you to function normally, it must be considered a serious illness. Most doctors, in fact, view anxiety as a condition that demands medical care *the moment the patient thinks it does.*

As one anxiety specialist says: "If a patient *thinks* he is suffering from excess anxiety, there is little doubt in my mind that he *really is.*"

In a sense, this attitude allows the anxiety victim to diagnose his or her own condition. Doctors are usually unwilling to accept self-diagnosis. With anxiety, the patient's own opinion may help them distinguish between everyday anxiety that will probably diminish without intervention, and more serious cases.

The Role of Drugs, Chemicals, Illness

As research on anxiety progresses, it becomes more evident that anxiety is as much an organic ailment as a psychological one. It is likely, experts say, that some anxiety symptoms—including panic attacks and phobias—result from subtle chemical changes within the brain. These can be caused, among other things, by everyday drugs or even substances common in the diets of many people.

Prescription drugs in carefully controlled dosages have recently proved very effective in the treatment of various kinds of anxieties, including agoraphobia and panic attacks. This, doctors believe, is further evidence that the chemical processes that occur naturally during times of stress may in many patients become disordered, and be directly responsible for causing serious, long-lasting anxieties.

As many as 40 percent of all those seeking treatment for anxiety (or depression, for that matter) may also suffer from significant physical disease. The reason for this may be either that untreated anxiety helped to cause the symptoms, or that an illness, for example heart disease, led to anxiety. A list of illnesses that are known frequently to cause anxiety appears in appendix B.

Diet, too, can play a role in anxiety. Heavy use of caffeine (more than ten cups of coffee daily) sometimes brings on anxiety. Monosodium glutamate, the cause of the so-called Chinese Restaurant Syndrome, can also trigger anxiety.

Some prescription, over-the-counter, and recreational drugs are known to cause anxiety. Among them are heart drugs such as digitalis; stimulants such as amphetamine; the arthritis medication Indocin; decongestants; antipsychotic drugs; and many others. A list of some of the commonly prescribed drugs linked to anxiety appears in appendix C.

Withdrawal from sedatives, opiates, or alcohol can also bring on serious anxiety attacks, as can the use of substances inhaled for recreation, including gasoline.

If you experience anxiety while taking any medication or recreational drug, tell your doctor about your experience. Changes in the dosage of a prescription drug, or sound advice about the use of recreational substances, can often eliminate the anxiety.

Personality and Heredity

Everyone's response to stress is different. The ability to deal effectively with anxiety-producing situations, and thus to overcome the anxiety's cause, is equally individualistic. It is each person's unique ability to cope with a situation that partially determines whether anxiety will change from a normal, healthy response into an illness.

The ability to handle stress well may in large measure be due to the way you were taught to manage unpleasant situations. If you learned to shrug off pressures on the job, they are less likely to cause anxiety.

The capacity to ward off anxiety may also be

related to the way those around you—family, colleagues, friends—deal with anxiety.

Children imitate those around them. If a child is raised in a household with someone who has a phobia, the child is at greater risk of himself developing a phobia. Anxiety often surfaces among members of the same family. When researchers studied the family of one phobia victim, they discovered that both parents had signs of the disorder and two sisters were seriously phobic as well.

Emotional trauma—a frightening experience that produces intense emotion—may also cause anxiety. An attack by a dog during childhood, for example, can in adulthood result in a fear of dogs, and even of other animals only vaguely similar to dogs.

Researchers have also found that some people may be prone genetically to excessive anxiety. Agoraphobia (the fear of leaving a safe place and visiting open spaces) and the closely related panic attacks, which seem to result in part from unusual chemical activity within the brain, are almost certainly partly genetic in origin; some 30% of all cases are shared by close family members.

Increased knowledge about the causes of anxiety, especially when biological in origin, is good news for victims. Biological disorders generally respond well to medication, and once a biological factor is established, the search for more effective drugs can begin.

5.

TREATING ANXIETY

- *Accurate diagnosis is essential to proper treatment*
- *Treatment differs for varying kinds of anxiety*
- *Drugs and therapy together are often effective*

Treating anxiety may be as simple as changing the dosage of a drug found to cause it. But usually treatment is much more complex.

The first step is to diagnose the illness.

The second is to determine its intensity.

Unlike diagnosing a heart ailment or a kidney malfunction—where X-rays or other tests may show the problem quite clearly—diagnosing anxiety depends on the patient's perception of his or her illness. Most doctors believe that if the anxiety is felt strongly enough for the patient to seek medical attention, it is probably severe enough to warrant treatment.

A large part of a doctor's diagnosis focuses on eliminating possible causes that can be quickly dealt with, such as poor diet, physical illness, or certain medications that cause anxiety.

The decision on treatment requires a doctor's understanding of how seriously the patient's life is being affected. Is it influencing his or her job, or leading to poor business decisions? Causing problems at home? Forcing a change in lifestyle?

A physician might advise a person who has mild, generalized anxiety, and who is not seriously bothered by it, to forego medications and seek counseling instead.

Behavior therapy or behavior modification—aimed at changing the patient's responses to anxiety-producing situations—might be recommended, particularly for phobic disorders.

This may involve *relaxation* and/or *desensitization* treatment, which teaches people to allow their muscles to relax as they are gradually brought into increasingly closer contact with the source of anxiety, the "stimulus." It calls for diversion from the stimulus as soon as the anxiety appears, and for a return to the stimulus after the anxiety subsides. Usually, steady reassurance that nothing harmful will happen is a part of this type of treatment.

People who are afraid to board airplanes, for instance, might visit an airport and tour an airplane, with a pilot or mechanic as their guide, to help overcome the anxiety by learning about aircraft safety measures. They are brought closer and closer to the airplane, periodically fighting the buildup of anxiety, until eventually they feel comfortable sitting in a passenger seat and imagining themselves on a flight.

A variation of this type of behavior therapy is *exposure treatment* or *flooding*. It forces the patient to confront the anxiety-causing situation, or the object of the phobia, for as long as possible *despite being almost overcome by anxiety.* Through a steady increase of the exposure time until it is longer than any the patient will ever have to face in "real life" situations, many people have learned to handle their anxiety. The procedure tries to bring the anxiety victim to the very edge of a panic attack but without inducing one.

These therapies rely on the observation that severe anxiety, including panic attacks, requires a lot of energy as the heart beats faster, muscles flex, and perspiration increases. The body, therapists know, cannot sustain such an energy output for very long without pausing to recover. Therapists take advantage of every brief recovery period to provide reassurance and to help prepare the patient for another confrontation with the cause of his or her anxiety.

Treatments that directly expose the anxiety victim to the cause of his or her anxiety—under carefully controlled conditions—have been known to cure the illness within months or weeks—sometimes even days. While widespread publicity may attend these "miracle" cures, they do not work for everyone, and should be attempted only under a doctor's direction.

Group therapy with other current and former victims of anxiety often is part of a treatment program. During group therapy, discussions can bring about increased understanding of the illness and generate hope that it can be conquered.

Psychotherapy, which assumes that anxiety is rooted in emotional difficulties and personality problems, focuses on overcoming anxiety through in-depth discussions of the patient's past. It, too, is included in many treatment programs.

Drug Treatment

The use of drugs to treat anxiety and the relative effectiveness of one drug over another are subjects of widespread dispute among specialists. Many drugs are of little or no proven benefit in the treatment of anxiety. They are nevertheless still commonly prescribed.

Several drugs, however, are known to reduce severe anxiety, limit or eliminate panic attacks, and help overcome phobias more rapidly.

WORKING WITH YOUR DOCTOR

Follow the treatment course your doctor recommends. That means taking your medication as prescribed, and actively participating in any therapy program that may be recommended.

If you are unhappy about the results of the treatment, speak with your doctor. Get another opinion if you wish, but don't stop your treatment on your own.

Learn as much as you can about anxiety, its causes, and its treatment. Knowledge is one key to dealing successfully with anxiety.

The most effective treatment for most kinds of anxiety appears to be a combination of drugs and behavior-modification therapy or psychotherapy. In instances when the drugs merely help to calm down the patient, they may simultaneously provide an opportunity for other treatment methods to start working.

Some studies of at least one kind of anxiety—agoraphobia—show that about one third of all patients recover using medication alone, another third also require short-range supportive therapy, and another third need long-term therapy.

Tranquilizers and sedatives are routinely prescribed for certain types of anxiety. Many of them have been notably successful. These drugs include a family of medications called benzodiazepines, which includes Valium, Librium, and Dalmane, as well as barbiturates and meprobamate.

Benzodiazepines are considered the "first choice" antianxiety drugs. They are less dangerous than barbiturates and meprobamate, cause fewer side effects, and have a lower risk of creating addiction or dependence.

The benzodiazepines, although far safer than barbiturates, nevertheless remain somewhat dangerous, mainly because of a potential for addiction. They are generally prescribed for limited periods and often as one part of an overall treatment program. All benzodiazepines are equally effective in treating anxiety, but each takes effect at a different speed, remains effective in the body for a different length of time, and is metabolized differently (so one may be selected over another according to an individual's unique ability to handle the drug).

Most tranquilizers and sedatives seem to be of little benefit, however, in the treatment of phobias, panic attacks, or obsessive-compulsive anxiety. These three ailments are now sometimes treated with antidepressant drugs, which research shows may be more effective than many tranquilizers. Among these drugs are the new benzodiazepine alprazolam, the tricyclic antidepressants, including imipramine and closely related medications, which seem to block spontaneous panic, as well as monoamine oxidase inhibitors, especially phenelzine.

By altering neurochemical activity deep within the brain, these drugs in effect raise the victim's panic threshold. They are prescribed cautiously because of their potential side effects.

One new drug with great promise for the treatment of anxiety, but still under investigation, is Buspirone, the first in a new family of chemicals known as azaspirodecanediones. Unlike some other antianxiety drugs, Buspirone appears to cause sleepiness only at high doses, is nonaddictive, and may have fewer overall adverse effects. Its use in treating panic attacks has not been well studied.

6.

DEPRESSION—WHAT IS IT?

• *Depression encompasses a wide variety of disorders*
• *Its victims suffer enormously, sometimes for months or years*
• *Like many other illnesses, depression can be treated*

Depression is a word we hear a lot today. It is commonly used to describe those feelings brought on by an enormous variety of unpleasant events, ranging from a bad day at the office to a state of tense global relationships.

A high-school basketball player, after losing an important game, might be heard to exclaim: "I'm *so* depressed." Similarly, an office manager might put down his newspaper to announce: "All these crime stories are so *depressing*."

Or we use words like *sad* or *blue* to describe our feelings. Newspapers print articles about "post-holiday blues," or "December depression," every year.

Depression can, indeed, be merely a passing "down" mood based on the day's—even the moment's—bad news. The basketball player wins the next game, the manager institutes a profitable company policy, and the depression lifts.

A few days after we were convinced that everything was awful, things suddenly start to look better. Life becomes fun again. Experts call this "self-limiting depression," and are loath to treat it with drugs or therapy. It is, in a word, normal.

Sometimes depression takes weeks or months to ebb, for example following the death of a family member. However, it usually disappears.

In many cases, though, depression holds on to its victims tenaciously, refusing to let go even after several months. Years can pass without depression loosening its grip. It can become a constant state of apathy requiring medical treatment.

Doctors use the word *depression* to describe many disorders that affect people's moods. Differences in how serious they are, and how long they last, distinguish one kind of depression from another. Their causes also set them apart, as do the particular ways they are experienced by their victims.

Depression, then, is many illnesses. If short-lived—such as the feeling a teenager might have when waiting in vain for that special phone call—it seldom requires medical attention. An understanding family—and, at last, the right phone call—is usually all the "treatment" required.

In this book we are focusing on depression serious enough to warrant professional care. An estimated ten million Americans are believed to suffer from such serious depression, and experts think many more cases go unrecognized. Depression has been called "the common cold" of disorders involving the mind and mood. But depression is much more dangerous than a common cold. It is a public-health problem of staggering proportions.

Prolonged Depression Is an Illness

Depression is considered a major illness when it takes the form of a prominent and persistent mood disturbance, and has symptoms that persist for at least two weeks, occurring nearly every day.

In other words, major depression is no longer a short "passage" between two lengthy periods of happiness and enthusiasm. It is instead a near-constant feeling of helplessness that, without treatment, greatly reduces the likelihood of the victim's life ever returning to normal.

This type of depression separates its victims from reality, causes their thoughts to focus on doom or death, and leads many to contemplate suicide.

Depression has plagued people throughout history. Here and in other countries it is variously known as melancholia, *Weltschmerz* (sickness of the world), *mal du siècle* (sickness of the century), and despair. Abraham Lincoln experienced severe depression; so did Queen Elizabeth I, Sigmund Freud, Winston Churchill, and generations of writers and artists. In the thirteenth century, Thomas Aquinas described depression as *tristitia de spirituali bono* (sorrow about spiritual well-being).

Until recently, victims had to fight their illness without medical care, in the face of the popular misconception that depression was a purely mental illness. That error persists today, incorrectly branding depressed people as "crazy" and attaching a social stigma to the illness.

Yet a great many fast, effective treatments are now available, since in the past two decades as much has been learned about depression's causes and cures as in all previous recorded history. In fact, depression victims today find that with the help of drugs and/or therapy, they often feel better within weeks of starting treatment.

A REALISTIC VIEW OF DEPRESSION

• *Depression is an illness often rooted in biological or genetic factors.*

• *Depression can be successfully treated. New research into the origins of depression, new diagnostic techniques, new drugs, and better use of all drugs—as well as new types of short-term psychotherapies—have led to major treatment breakthroughs.*

• *Depression can strike children, teens, and men and women of all ages and in all walks of life.*

• *Depression is exceptionally common. About 25 percent of all Americans experience severe depression at some time during their lives. About 10 million Americans may be suffering some form of the illness at this moment.*

Fully 80 percent of all people suffering from major depression can be helped. We have come a long way since the days when "melancholia" victims were doomed to lifetimes of black moods, and physically wasted away because they took no joy in eating, sleeping, or maintaining their health.

Depression demands the right treatment, just as any other illness does. Decades of research demonstrate that the different kinds of depression respond best to different treatments. The differences are due in part to the multiple origins of depression, which are still the subject of intense study. Some depressions have biological roots, and may indeed be carried in families by genes. Depression can also reflect the interaction between stress and biological factors.

Depression can be caused by chemical imbalances affecting those parts of the brain that control pleasure. It can also be a symptom of physical illness, just as a fever can be a symptom of an infection.

ARE YOU DEPRESSED?

Doctors use a variety of methods to discover whether their patients are depressed. A thorough medical history must be taken, and should include information on whether any relatives have faced the illness. A complete physical checkup is essential before depression is diagnosed.

Among the tools for spotting depression are question-and-answer or multiple-choice tests given to those who show signs of the illness. Some tests were created so that doctors can question their patients in person and note the answers. In other tests, the patient answers a series of written questions and submits a completed response form to the doctor for evaluation.

The Beck Depression Inventory, developed by Dr. Aron T. Beck of the University of Pennsylvania Medical School, is one multiple-choice test frequently used by doctors. Each topic—such as sadness, guilt, or irritability—offers four statements, ranging in value from 0 to 3. A patient indicates which statement best describes his or her feelings at that moment. For example, statements about your "sense of failure" offer these alternatives:

0. I do not feel like a failure.
1. I feel I have failed more than the average person.
2. As I look back on my life all I can see are a lot of failures.
3. I feel I am a complete failure as a person.

Another popular depression test called the Self-rating Depression Scale offers a range of possible responses to 20 statements, with each response carrying a different score. For example, the statement "I am more irritable than usual" can be answered "None (or a little) of the time," "Some of the time," "A good part of the time" or "Most of the time." If you answered "Most of the time," you scored 4; "Some of the time" has 2 points.

With these and similar tests, scores are added up when the test is completed. A low score indicates you are probably not depressed, while higher scores point to an increasing likelihood that you are, and may even show the degree of your depression.

Among the topics commonly included in tests for depression:

Sadness. Do you feel sad, "down-hearted," or "blue"? How often? Are you unable to snap out of it?

Optimism/Pessimism. Do you feel your future is bright? Or are things so bad that it seems they can never improve?

Success/Failure. Do you feel successful? Or does it seem your life has been a long series of failures?

Satisfaction. Does your life seem full? Do you still enjoy doing the things you always enjoyed?

Or have you become dissatisfied and bored with everything?

Guilt. Do you feel guilty about things? How often, and how seriously?

Punishment. Do you expect to be punished for something?

Self-Attitude. Do you like yourself—or feel disappointed or disgusted with yourself? Do you hate yourself?

Self-Criticism. Are you critical of yourself? How much do you blame yourself for any weaknesses, mistakes, or faults?

Self-Destruction. Have you contemplated suicide? How seriously have you considered it?

Daily Rhythm. Do you feel better in the morning or in the evening? Do things always seem to go downhill through the day?

Eating Habits. Are you eating better than before, or have you lost your interest in food?

Physical Health. Does your heart seem to beat faster than it used to? Are you losing weight? Do you have digestive problems, such as constipation? Are you so restless you can't seem to keep still? Do you get tired for no reason?

Social Contact. Are you still interested in other people? How much? Has there been a change in your interest in sex? Do you feel useful to others, and needed?

Sleeping Pattern. Do you sleep soundly? Or are you restless at night? Have you been waking up early?

Crying. How often do you cry? More than you used to, or less? Are things so bad that you can't even cry any more?

Irritability. Do you find yourself getting annoyed or irritated by things that never used to bother you? Or are you no longer bothered by things that used to annoy you?

Mental Alertness. Does it seem your mind is as clear as it used to be?

Decision Making. Are decisions easy for you, or difficult? Has there been a change in the way you make decisions?

No single question is enough to show that you are depressed. Your answers to some test questions, even though they may seem negative, could have other explanations. For instance, you might be losing weight and getting tired quickly not because of depression, but because you are on a diet; you might be sleeping poorly because your neighbors are unusually noisy at night.

The tests, which should be conducted by your doctor, rely on your answers being as truthful as possible. Physicians have found that written tests often provide more information than would be gained by personal discussions with their patients. During a doctor's interview people sometimes give answers they think will "please" the doctor, but they might be more honest when completing a test form. Additionally, doctors can use the results of written tests to help diagnose ailments other than depression that may be bothering their patients.

7.

THE MANY FACES OF DEPRESSION

- *There are numerous types of depression*
- *Depression can stem from biological, environmental or hereditary causes*
- *All depressions can produce distinct physical and emotional symptoms*

Through the years, specialists have given a variety of names to different types of depression, depending on the causes of each type and the ways the types most often manifest themselves. A diagnostic manual often used by physicians, the DSM III, outlines specific symptoms of depression and assigns identifying names to each type of depression.

Sometimes, however, depression doesn't fit neatly into any one category. Researchers continually expand our knowledge of depression, and the classifications listed here are constantly changing and overlapping in the technical debates among doctors.

Some major categories of recognized depression types are:

Primary. The depression itself is the illness, as opposed to depression being a symptom of some other illness.

Secondary. The depression is the result of a medical illness, a psychiatric disorder, or environmental factors.

Dysthymic (neurotic). A low mood that may last for years, with temporary periods of feeling better. It may be related to environmental factors; sometimes it is characterized by anxiety and persistent trouble in dealing with other people. While dysthymic depression may appear extremely serious to its victims, it seldom requires medical treatment.

Major. The depression lasts for several weeks or longer, and frequently recurs. It interrupts normal lifestyle through many symptoms, often somatic (bodily) ones.

Reactive (situational, exogenous, normal, grieving). Depression caused by some stressful situation, such as the death of a spouse. Reactive depression usually disappears with the removal of the stress-causing situation, or gets better as time passes, often on its own.

Biologic (endogenous, autonomous). Depression caused by a biochemical or genetic factor, or illness. Biologic depression can arise regardless of events, or can be precipitated by them. It can come on either slowly or suddenly without warning, can last for weeks, months, or longer, and may recur. The term is sometimes used to describe major depression.

Unipolar. Periods of depression occurring in cycles, alternating with periods of normal (not manic) mood.

Bipolar (manic, mood swings). Depression occurring in cycles, alternating with periods of mania. In the manic phase, a person feels "on top of the world." But the symptoms of hyperactivity and elation can become uncontrollable. The high excitement or euphoria is often followed by severe depression. People suffering from mild mood swings are frequently very high achievers. However, the mania can escalate out of control, until there is a "crash." After a manic episode, a victim may be ruined financially because of reckless spending. Generally, the manic phase is briefer than the depressive one. Each cycle can be as short as forty-eight hours or as long as a year.

Involutional. Depression occurring during middle and late-middle life and associated with menopause in women, and andropause in men. Involutional depression is linked to changes in hormonal activity and to worry about dwindling sexual and work capacities. The term is used less often since research has shown similar depression occurs among younger people.

Masked. The depression is hidden from the victim and everyone else—including the doctor—behind pain complaints, physical illness, or anxiety. Masked depression often results in the treatment's being directed at the apparent illness, for instance stomach trouble or headaches, while the depression itself remains untreated. If no medical cause for physical symptoms can be found, or if as soon as one physical illness is cured another replaces it, depression should be considered as a possible underlying cause.

Underlying. Depression afflicting nearly half of all alcoholics, who may have first resorted to alcohol in an attempt to cure their depression. May compound a serious drinking problem.

Double. Double depression is a chronic state of dysthymic (mild) depression with episodes of major depression. The severe episodes can last up to a year, and can recur.

Psychotic. An exceptionally serious disorder, often accompanied by a loss of contact with reality and delusions. In most cases, psychotic depression requires hospital care.

Effects of Depression

Symptoms of depression can range from such general problems as tiredness and vague pains, to specific conditions such as constipation, blurred vision, and impotence. They may also include the inability to enjoy hobbies, frequent crying spells, and difficulty in thinking clearly.

Recognizing depression, whether it strikes you or someone you know, can be extremely difficult. The illness can disguise itself by taking on one or more physical characteristics. Additionally, a host of emotional symptoms associated with depression can be very confusing. The symptoms of depression can bewilder doctors, as well as a victim's family. In general, all types of depression share the same symptoms, but the levels of severity, and how long the symptoms last, vary a great deal.

HOW DEPRESSION AFFECTS BODY AND MIND

Physical Symptoms

• *General: fatigue; tiredness; sleep disturbances (staying asleep, or waking up early); insomnia; skin problems.*

• *Pain: headache; stiff neck; heartburn; pains of the neck, chest, breast, ear, stomach, abdomen, shoulder, arm, leg, and lower back.*

• *Digestive system: loss of appetite and weight loss; increased appetite and weight gain; constipation; diarrhea; indigestion; nausea.*

• *Other: impotence.*

Emotional/Psychological Symptoms

• *Behavior: can't enjoy things as much as before (good food, a beautiful landscape, sex); less interested in family, friends, work, hobbies, pets; loss of initiative and ambition; increased apathy; crying spells; screaming; irritability; excessive complaints about minor things; agitated behavior.*

• *Mood: sadness; despondence; pessimism; sense of impending doom; future seems "hopeless"; sense of fear or anxiety; self-reproach or guilt feelings; drop of self-esteem; feelings of inadequacy, self-dislike, and helplessness.*

• *Thought patterns: difficulty in thinking clearly, remembering, concentrating; thoughts confused; thoughts of death, contemplation of suicide.*

• *Relations with others: feelings of rejection (some possibly real, due to depressed behavior); withdrawal from activities.*

8.

CAUSES OF DEPRESSION

- *Physical illness can cause depression*
- *Prescription and recreational drugs can also be responsible*
- *Age and personality can play a role as well*

Depression does not have one single cause, but has many different ones, as mentioned earlier. It can result from external events or can stem from subtle biochemical changes within us. Environmental—sometimes called depression "mimickers"—genetic, and psychological factors can all play a role, either together or individually. As with many illnesses, knowing about the causes is the first step toward conquering depression.

Physical Illness

Nearly any physical illness can trigger a limited degree of depression. It is a normal, entirely appropriate response to the loss of health and the danger of disease. Such depression usually will resolve itself with little or no treatment, most rapidly when the illness is cured.

Some illnesses, however, cause more severe depression, which can become a long-lasting condition that may grow worse unless recognized and treated. Among the illnesses known to trigger serious depression are stroke, arthritis, cancer, and various degenerative diseases. A list of illnesses often associated with depression appears in appendix D.

Medical Procedures and Accidents

Depression can precede or follow surgery, especially such operations as mastectomy, hysterectomy, or sterilization procedures. Medical treatment such as chemotherapy, or accidents that leave their victims disfigured or physically impaired, can also cause major depression. In all these instances the individual's life or sense of identity may be significantly affected.

Depression can also result from high levels of chronic pain, such as lower-back pain.

Diet

Caffeine addiction—drinking more than ten cups of coffee or tea daily, for instance—can cause depression. So, too, can diseases related to poor nutrition.

Some of the foods we all eat regularly recently have been linked to depression. Sensitivity among some people to yeast or sugar are two examples. Yeast is found in most baked goods, as well as in cheese, alcoholic beverages, pickled or fermented foods, mushrooms, and dried fruits.

The amino acids in certain foods are also suspected triggers of depression in those who are particularly sensitive to them.

Drugs

Hundreds of drugs can cause depression. These include prescription drugs (including some used to treat high blood pressure) as well as many used for recreation (including alcohol).

It is not always clear how drugs cause depression. Some drugs appear to change the chemical balance within areas of the brain where mood and emotion are controlled. With others, it is not known how they act to bring about, or encourage, depression.

Whenever a sense of depression coincides with the start of a new medication, the doctor who prescribed the medicine should be told immediately. A list of drugs known to cause depression appears in appendix E.

Drug Withdrawal

Reducing the use of alcohol and/or stimulants—including amphetamine, cocaine, methylphenidate, phenmetrazine—can cause major depression, as can total withdrawal from alcohol and/or recreational drugs. Generally, the depression resulting from alcohol withdrawal lasts less than three weeks.

Loss and Grief

Depression is often caused by a significant loss, or a major change in one's life status. The loss can be the death of a loved one, being fired from a job, the breakup of a close relationship, a business failure, retirement, or financial losses.

Grieving—mourning for a person, pet, or anything we valued that is suddenly gone—is a normal outlet for the emotions generated by loss. Intense grief over a loss tends to come in waves, and the more important the lost person, object, or situation was, the more intense the periods of grieving will be.

Grieving follows a progression of physical and psychological stages including anxiety, irritability, guilt feelings, and withdrawal. The process—often highly ritualized—allows us to find a way to restructure our lives and to find a new sense of completeness.

Depression is often a part of grieving. Sometimes it lasts much longer than it should, and causes serious difficulties if not treated. Depression can also result when people don't have the opportunity to mourn a loss.

Age

From infancy to old age, depression can strike anyone, at any time. No age group is immune, a fact illustrated by the age distribution of a group of 154 depressed patients at the time their illness was diagnosed:

Age in years	11–20	21–30	31–40	41–50	51–60	61–70	71–80
Number of patients	6	14	22	26	39	29	18

Among people ages 26–40, depression is often the reactive or situational type, usually triggered by a job loss, a move to a new home, a death in the family, or a child leaving home. People aged 45–60 more often encounter endogenous depression; here, environmental factors may not be as easily identified, leaving genetic or biochemical factors as likely contributing causes.

Children from infancy to teens can experience depression just as adults do. In recent years, depression has been recognized as the underlying cause of many behavioral and developmental problems among youngsters.

Childhood depression is exceptionally difficult to diagnose, partly because children experience such a range of conflicting emotions and partly because they cannot always accurately describe their feelings.

However, changes in behavior and attitude are often clues to depression.

Apathy, irritability, and hyperactivity are common signs of depression. Children who cry a lot, refuse to eat, are accident-prone, run away, steal, and/or abuse alcohol or drugs may be depressed. If a youngster plays the role of class bully or clown in school, or performs poorly and has trouble learning, depression may be the cause. Other symptoms may include irritability and difficulty getting going in the morning.

Like adults, children suffering from depression often become listless, joyless, helpless, anxious, isolated, and self-absorbed. They quarrel, and they complain about physical aches and emotional hurts.

Considering that many of these signs of depression can also be normal aspects of growing up, it is easy to understand a doctor's difficulty in diagnosing depression. That difficulty is compounded after a diagnosis is made.

Many children react to antidepressant drugs in the exact opposite way as do adults. A medication that lifts an adult out of depression may sink a child deeper into a black mood. Some children, on the other hand, require higher antidepressant doses than adults before any effect is evident. And drugs that intensify depression among adults sometimes lift children out of depression.

Behavioral changes in your child should be discussed with your pediatrician or family doctor. Pay particular attention to a usually happy child who suddenly becomes withdrawn and unresponsive, or a bright, neat student whose performance falls and who neglects personal appearance.

Among teenagers, depression is an important factor in at least two-thirds of all suicides. In the United States, suicide is now the second leading cause of death during the teen years.

Although the elderly are extremely vulnerable to depression, age is not the key factor. Instead, depression among senior citizens is often the reactive type, tied to major events in their lives, such as the death of a spouse or close friend, dwindling financial resources, or poor physical or mental health.

Depression among the elderly may also be caused by feelings of abandonment by family members, or a sense that their lives are almost over and they are therefore worthless.

Many instances of depression among senior citizens are due directly to the drugs prescribed for their physical ailments. In some cases, the depression may lift as soon as the medication or its dosage is changed.

Sex

Two-thirds of all Americans diagnosed as suffering from depression are women.

This may be due partly to the fact that women visit their doctors more often than men, and thus make up more of the statistics. Also, women may be more open about their feelings than are men, resulting in a higher rate of diagnoses. Hormonal differences may also be responsible to some degree for women's suffering more frequently from depression.

Some physicians contend that these statistics are flawed by bias within a male-dominated mental-health establishment. While there may be some truth to this belief, it is unlikely that bias alone could make such significant differences in the numbers.

In fact, recent studies show that the reasons actually may stem in part from the biological and cultural role allotted to women, who are often conditioned from infancy to remain dependent. Eventually, this may foster a need for the approval of others greater than that among men; such a feeling is often linked to depression.

Biochemical

Freud, the founding father of psychoanalysis, was a neurologist by profession. While he recognized that some depressions have biological roots, he also found that many patients had no known physical basis for their symptoms. He eventually arrived at a concept that tied depression to events in an individual's past, many of which were long-forgotten.

From Freud's time until recently, depression was

treated for the most part as a purely mental disorder. Other than shock therapy, the only treatments widely available were psychoanalysis and psychotherapy, originating from Freud's studies.

Results of the Freudian treatment were mixed; while some people recovered from depression through psychoanalysis, most didn't. At the time, of course, no causes for or explanations of depression were known.

A radical change occurred when depression started to be addressed not as a purely psychological disorder but as a range of illnesses, in many cases caused by physiological factors—such as abnormal chemistry within the nervous system (especially the brain), and genetic predisposition.

It has been found that people suffering from mild depression show a consistent pattern of decreased metabolism within the brain, and that metabolic rates correspond to mood and behavioral changes. Researchers theorize that significant reductions in the brain's metabolic rates affect those areas involving mood control, fear, anger, and other strong emotions, as well as logic and reasoning.

Various chemical imbalances in the brain almost certainly can cause depression, and a wide range of substances are being closely studied to determine their roles in influencing moods and emotions.

For example, acetylcholine, serotonin, and norepinephrine are substances in the brain that transmit signals from one nerve cell to another, including nerve impulses that regulate mood. Researchers are trying to learn how these and other neurotransmitters perform their jobs and precisely what roles they play in depression.

One theory now being studied associates depression with a naturally occurring substance within our bodies called 2-phenylethylamine (PEA), which appears to play a crucial role in emotional health.

Lowered amounts of PEA in the brain, the theory suggests, may cause depression.

While many findings from such research are still tentative, it is clear that some forms of depression can be pinpointed by tests performed on the body's various glands—hypothalmus, pituitary, adrenal—which regulate hormones and other chemicals.

Genetic

It is likely that depression is sometimes related, at least in part, to a faulty gene. But having a genetic predisposition does not mean someone will become depressed, only that the person will be susceptible to depression if other factors fall into place.

If a child who is genetically prone to depression learns at an early age how to cope with adversity, he or she may be less likely to become depressed when older. On the other hand, one who did not learn to deal effectively with problems may experience deep depression at any time. Studies show that about one in ten children of seriously depressed parents eventually develops depression.

Seasons

Science has recently confirmed what folklore has asserted for centuries: sunlight directly affects mood and mental functioning.

For many people, the short days of late fall and winter bring on listlessness and mild depression.

For others, the short days trigger severe, debilitating depression known as seasonal affective disorder (SAD). Its victims sleep fitfully, become sad and irritable, and lose their energy and libido. They retain, though, a hearty appetite; foods high in carbohydrates are eaten with gusto, and eating binges are frequent.

This disorder may be linked to the pineal gland at the base of the brain, which secretes the hormone melatonin during hours of darkness. The hormone seems to affect mood and mental agility.

Already, a treatment for SAD has proved effective for some people. When SAD victims are subjected to very bright lights in the morning and evening throughout the winter—in effect, lengthening the day—their pineal glands are "fooled" into producing more melatonin.

Pilot studies are under way to learn more about the effect of seasonal changes on depression, and whether seasonal depression is closely related to other forms of depression.

Sleep

Sleep disorders are a common result of depression and may also be a cause. People suffering from major depression enter the rapid eye movement (REM) phase of sleep, much sooner than do nondepressed individuals.

Furthermore, people who do not sleep well are more susceptible to becoming depressed.

Social Environment

The social environment is known to lead sometimes to depression. Members of racial, social, or economic groups with little chance of improving their status frequently experience hopelessness and low self-esteem, which are often the precursors of major depression. Moreover, stressful family situations, such as unhappy marriages, may result in depression in one or more family members.

Depression and Suicide

Suicide is the tenth leading cause of death among adults, and the second most significant among college students and adolescents, according to recent government figures. Statistically, homosexuals face a higher risk of suicide than do heterosexuals. About twenty-eight thousand people yearly kill themselves in the United States.

Depression is a factor in at least two-thirds of all suicides.

Drug and alcohol abuse are also contributing factors in suicides. Depressed people frequently try to alleviate their moods by turning to drugs and alcohol. This attempt at "self-medication" is actually counterproductive, since alcohol and many drugs contribute to depression.

Those who have never suffered from depression probably cannot understand the degree of futility and despondency faced by its victims. Depression is so all-encompassing and so psychologically painful that, for many, death seems the only way to cope with the illness.

Among victims of major depression, one warning sign is a sudden improvement for no apparent reason. The individual may have decided to commit suicide, and the signs of improvement may stem from the person's relief at knowing that the pain of depression is about to end.

It is *not true* that those who talk about suicide never carry out their plans. The fact is that most depressed people who killed themselves gave some prior indication of their plans, and the vast majority of suicides sought help prior to killing themselves.

Direct warnings are not the only clues to impending suicide. Indirect verbal warnings may include such statements as: "I don't think I'll be here next week."

Changes in behavior may also provide clues. Giving away all possessions and writing a will may be indications that suicide is being contemplated.

Previous suicide attempts provide the most important indications of actual intent to commit suicide.

Suicides among depressives often occur when a person is entering, or coming out of, a major bout of depression, since it is during these phases that the victim has the energy to complete the act.

The early-morning hours are common times for suicides, because depression victims generally wake up earlier than those they live with, are alone for hours, and feel worse in the early morning.

Whenever someone gives any clue whatsoever that suicide is being considered, the possibility should be taken seriously. Most cities have twenty-four-hour hotlines (often listed under "Suicide," "Crisis Intervention," "Helpline," or "Hotline" in phone books) where understanding experts can discuss suicidal thoughts with callers and help them through their crises. In addition, many hospital emergency rooms provide emergency psychiatric help.

9.

HELP AND TREATMENT FOR DEPRESSION

- *Knowing about depression is the first step to being helped*
- *Diagnosis is the key to treatment*
- *Results of treatment can be rapid and lasting*

Doctors sometimes have difficulty prescribing the best treatment for depression because symptoms can be so similar among different varieties of the illness. Medications that alleviate one kind of depression may have little or no effect on another; therapy that helps one person may not help the next, even when it appears that their depressions are virtually identical. One tool used by many physicians is the Beck Depression Inventory, a test given to patients who may be depressed. The test, which appears on pp. 38–41, provides doctors with some of the information necessary to make the proper diagnosis or rate the severity of the illness.

There are many common threads—even among dramatically different kinds of depression—which allow for several generalities about the treatment of depression. For instance, vital to any victim is the need to adopt a realistic view about the illness based on hard facts, not guesses or half-truths.

Helping Yourself

Several steps can be taken by those who are feeling depressed, have been diagnosed as suffering from depression, or who wonder if what they feel is, in fact, depression.

1. If you think you suffer from depression, you owe it to yourself to seek advice about the illness. Talk to your doctor, close family members, or religious advisers. Or contact your community's mental-health facility about diagnosis and treatment. Many hospitals have facilities for treatment or can provide information about where it can be obtained.

2. Learn all you can about depression and its treatment, so that you can ask your doctor the questions important to you and can more easily understand the answers.

3. Don't hide your depression behind a wall of silence. Others can help you, but first they must know of your illness.

4. Talk to others suffering from depression. Depressives Anonymous is one nationwide program, and many other self-help groups exist around the country.

5. Give the treatment a chance to work. After a month or two, if you feel there is no change in your condition, speak with your doctor. Seek a second opinion if you feel it might be helpful.

6. Be aware that your depression might follow a classic pattern. Sometime *after* your treatment

has started, you may experience a low point, and from there slowly begin to feel better. That's why you should stay with the treatment for several weeks before deciding whether it is improving your condition.

7. Tell your doctor about any bothersome, unusual, or disturbing emotions you're feeling. Some depression victims say they worry about hurting others or themselves, or feel they are "going crazy." These feelings can be extremely disturbing, but they can usually be treated—if your physician knows about them.

8. Recognize that suicide is a major risk faced by those suffering from depression. If you find yourself thinking about suicide, give your life *another ten minutes*. Use the ten minutes to call one of the nation's many twenty-four-hour hotlines, usually listed in telephone books under "Suicide." Their experienced professionals can give you genuine reason to hope for improvement and to plan for the future. Also, inform your physician of suicidal feelings; don't try to hide them.

Help from Family and Friends

Family members and friends can provide important help by not letting the depressed person withdraw into isolation. They can keep the individual active and busy, which will speed recovery once treatment begins. Some of the steps they can take:

1. Be willing to listen. Allow the depressed individual to say what's on his or her mind. Demonstrate love and understanding. Show interest in the person and concern about the illness. Bear in mind that depression can be treated, but treatment may take a long time.

2. Remember that neither the victim, nor the family, nor friends are at fault. Depression can strike anyone.

3. Depression is not a "voluntary" illness, nor is it a ploy to gain sympathy.

4. Be alert to some form of deception from the depressed person, who may try to cover up the illness—perhaps thinking it is socially "unacceptable." As the depression deepens, the coverup may become more elaborate. Again, be understanding about even this aspect of the illness.

What **Not** To Do

1. Don't encourage someone suffering from depression to "pull yourself together," or say things like: "You can snap out of it if you really want to." If that were possible, they would already have done so! Depression is extremely painful for its victims, who would like nothing more than to "snap out of it." But the "bootstrap" approach doesn't work, nor do most other do-it-yourself approaches. Insisting that depression victims are not in need of medical treatment only deepens their depression and further alienates them from their surroundings. It also exaggerates their feelings of guilt. They may become depressed about being depressed.

2. Don't turn away from the depressed person just because you think your help isn't adequate. Instead, openly admit that you feel you're not helping enough, and encourage the person to seek professional treatment.

3. Don't let a depressed person withdraw into isolation. Ask questions about the illness: "How do you feel? What are you worried about? What can I do to help?" Offer reassurances that treat-

ment is available and that it works. Explain that depression is often caused by a chemical imbalance in the body, and that medications are available to correct it.

4. Don't use what the depression victim says as ammunition for arguments or grounds for recriminations. Remember, depression is an illness over which an individual has little or no control. Again, try to persuade the person to seek professional help.

Today, many types of depression can be treated rapidly and effectively. Treatment can mean escape from a personal hell unthinkable to anyone who has never experienced major depression. In many cases, the best available treatment is drugs, sometimes in conjunction with therapy. The remarkable thing about drug treatment is that quite often it has an effect within a few weeks, and sometimes symptoms like insomnia are eased in days. The victim can experience joy and new energy very soon after the start of treatment.

Medical Treatment of Depression

Correct diagnosis is the key to proper medical treatment of depression.

Yet, diagnosis is difficult. Until recently, it was based almost solely on questioning the patient about himself. Now, new tests are available to measure such things as chemical changes in the brain, sleep patterns, and hormone levels.

In order to treat depression as effectively as possible, doctors must determine whether the depression has its roots in a biological condition or instead results from a major event in the victim's life. Some types of depression respond to certain drugs more readily than others, while some don't respond well to any drug treatment.

Drugs are not normally used to treat depression unless the illness is moderate to severe, and they are frequently prescribed in conjunction with some other form of therapy. Milder but more chronic types of depression sometimes respond well just to drugs, but are more commonly treated with psychotherapy.

For many years psychoanalysis and psychotherapy were the two kinds of "insight" therapy generally used to treat depression. In psychoanalysis, treatment focuses on the subconscious, with the analyst's personality kept out of view as the patient confronts past experiences. In psychotherapy, the therapist often confronts the patient with the immediate problem of living. Group, family, and gestalt therapies are forms of this treatment.

Both psychoanalysis and psychotherapy, however, often require more time to achieve results—often years—than most depressions last, even without medical treatment. Yet, both have their defenders, who insist that a depressed person has probably always been depressed and that therapy can help uncover and cure the underlying causes.

Recently, new forms of "insight" therapy have evolved. One is "brief psychotherapy," in many ways similar to the longer, more intensive form. It concentrates on the immediate situation believed to have led to the depression, based on the assumption that if the current situation is resolved, the individual can better cope with and overcome the depression.

Behavior therapy, another relatively new form of nondrug treatment, was developed especially to treat people suffering from depression.

One of its forms, "cognitive behavioral therapy," evolved during the past twenty years under the guidance of Dr. A. T. Beck and his colleagues at the University of Pennsylvania. Beck explains his theory of depression as "the notion that . . . thinking processes are diverted. Depressed people see things in a completely negative way. Positive events are just blotted out completely."

The aim of Dr. Beck's treatment is to teach people who are suffering from depression to change negative thoughts and perceptions of themselves. The therapist asks the patient to describe events that make him feel worthless, or a failure, then shows that other interpretations are possible.

Another form of behavior therapy, "interpersonal psychotherapy," was developed by Dr. Gerald Klerman of Massachusetts General Hospital, along with Dr. Myrna Weissman of Yale University and others in the New Haven–Boston Collaborative Depression Project. Interpersonal psychotherapy is based on the belief that depressed people have difficulty in getting along with others. Either the depression follows a disruption in relations with others, the theory holds, or the relations deteriorate as a result of the depression. In either instance, the aim of the therapy is to teach depressed individuals how to resolve conflicts in their relationships with others. By putting their relationships on a new basis, depression victims gain new control over their lives, improve their social functioning, and reduce the symptoms of their depression.

Such therapies together with drugs are the major current approaches to treating serious depression. For mild depression, therapy is often the only treatment needed.

Shock Therapy

Electroconvulsive therapy (ECT), commonly known as shock therapy, has been largely surpassed by drugs as a primary treatment for depression, but it is still used for those victims who have not been helped by drugs or who are unable to tolerate the side effects caused by the medications, and for those who are psychotic or on the verge of suicide. ECT can, with some patients, be both fast and effective, as well as less dangerous than drugs.

Advances in technology have resulted in a marked reduction in the dangers of ECT, during which the brain is briefly flooded with carefully calibrated electric shocks, which bring on controlled convulsions.

The procedure has graduated from the "horror chamber" status depicted in fiction to a useful treatment employing sophisticated medical equipment. Pretreatment administration of muscle-relaxing drugs and short-term anesthesia make ECT significantly less harrowing than it used to be. Often, a patient's only notable physical reaction to ECT is a curling of the toes or mild finger movements during treatment.

Sleep Deprivation Therapy

Depression caused by abnormal cycles in an individual's biological clock is sometimes lifted overnight by disruption of the patient's deep "rapid eye movement" (REM) sleep. Using brainwave measurements to indicate when REM sleep is about to begin, the sleeping person is awakened briefly; this process appears to reset the body's own clock. This therapy is carried out only in supervised settings, and its usefulness as an important treatment against depression has not yet been established.

Drugs

Antidepressant drugs are the treatment of choice for those suffering from major depression.

There were originally two major classes of drugs used to treat depression: monoamine oxidase inhibitors and tricyclic antidepressants. Lithium was added to the medical arsenal in the late 1960's, and is used primarily to treat bipolar depression.

New drugs are constantly being developed in an effort to help cure those who do not tolerate, or who are helped only slightly, by medications currently on the market.

Tricyclic antidepressants are in the forefront of drug treatment today. Some 70-80 percent of depression victims enjoy the complete elimination of their illness with one of these powerful medications. They generally require at least two weeks to lift depression, working through their chemical effect on the sections of the brain where emotional responses originate.

Drugs known as monoamine oxidase inhibitors, or MAO inhibitors, may be equally effective. They are generally prescribed for depressed people who exhibit symptoms that are the opposite of those common with depression: overeating rather than weight loss; oversleeping rather than insomnia. However, the drugs also work on some patients who exhibit classic symptoms. Those using MAO inhibitors must observe strict dietary guidelines.

Two new compounds, trazodone hydrochloride and nomifensine maleate, have been introduced recently. Their chemical structures and biological effects distinguish them from other antidepressants.

Manic-depressive illness is often treated with lithium-based drugs, which control pronounced mood swings. Some manic-depressives, however, require antidepressants at the same time. In lithium drug treatment, side effects and adverse effects are frequent. Because dosage levels are extremely important, frequent blood tests are essential in order to determine proper doses.

II

**The Most Commonly
Prescribed Anxiety and
Depression Drugs in the
United States, Generic and
Brand Names, with
Complete Descriptions
of Drugs and Their Effects**

GENERAL INFORMATION ABOUT DRUG TYPES

Following is general information about the different types of drugs commonly used to treat anxiety and depression. Specific information about your drug can be found in the next section, where drugs are listed alphabetically by their generic names (drugs that combine two medications are listed alphabetically by their brand names). If you have trouble locating your drug, please consult the index (p. 196). Because some of these drugs are potentially addictive, and others can cause dangerous side effects, do not let anyone else take your medication, and do not change your prescribed dosage without your doctor's approval. Many of the drugs listed here are especially dangerous to youngsters. **Keep all medications out of the reach of children.**

Barbiturates

Amobarbital (see p. 86)
Amobarbital Sodium (see p. 89)
Mephobarbital (see p. 143)

Barbiturates were first used medically in 1882, but were not widely marketed until the early 1900s. They appear to interfere with nerve impulses within the brain; small doses "calm the nerves," while larger doses can make you fall asleep.

Overdoses are extremely dangerous; they can lead to coma and death.

Barbiturates are potentially addictive. Long-term use of small doses, or brief use of large doses, can result in a buildup of tolerance, followed by withdrawal symptoms when the drugs are stopped.

In addition to their uses in controlling anxiety and as sleeping pills, barbiturates are also helpful in treating epileptic seizures.

Only your doctor can determine which (if any) barbiturate is best for you, and at what dosage level.

Benzodiazepines

Alprazolam (see p. 80)
Chlordiazepoxide Hydrochloride (see p. 96)
Clorazepate Dipotassium (see p. 99)
Diazepam (see p. 107)
Halazepam (see p. 117)

Lorazepam (see p. 137)
Oxazepam (see p. 154)
Prazepam (see p. 161)

Benzodiazepines are the most commonly prescribed tranquilizers in this country, and are often abused. Thousands of emergency-room visits yearly are due, at least in part, to misuse or abuse of these drugs.

The chemical structure of benzodiazepines was first discovered in 1933, but was viewed as insignificant. Then, in the 1950s, researchers learned that laboratory animals given one version of benzodiazepine were calmed down, or put to sleep, with doses that seemed to present little danger to the animals. Shortly afterward, tests on humans confirmed the benefits of benzodiazepines in treating anxiety, convulsions, insomnia, muscle tension, and alcohol withdrawal.

By directly affecting "receptor sites" in the brain, benzodiazepines make you either more tranquil or sleepier, depending on the strength of the drug and the amount you take. There appear to be few significant differences in over-all effect among the benzodiazepines. Some people may develop side effects from one of them but not from another, due to each person's unique response to small differences in the drugs' chemical structures, and to each person's metabolism.

Benzodiazepines are potentially addictive. Long-term use of small doses, or brief use of large doses, can result in a buildup of tolerance, followed by withdrawal symptoms when the drugs are stopped.

Only your doctor can determine which (if any) benzodiazepine is best for you and at what dosage level.

Other Antianxiety Drugs

Hydroxyzine Hydrochloride/Hydroxyzine
    Pamoate (see p. 120)
Meprobamate (see p. 145)

Hydroxyzine (hydrochloride and pamoate), an antihistamine, is believed to reduce anxiety by suppressing electrical and/or chemical activity in part of the brain.

Meprobamate, derived from the carbamate drug family, has its antianxiety effects in the thalamus and limbic systems and throughout the brain. It is less widely used than benzodiazepines due to its more limited safety margin.

Only your doctor can determine whether one of these drugs should be a part of your treatment and, if so, what dosage levels should be used.

Tri-, Quadra- and Tetracyclic Antidepressants

Amitriptyline Hydrochloride (see p. 83)
Amoxapine (see p. 91)
Desipramine Hydrochloride (see p. 104)
Doxepin Hydrochloride (see p. 110)
Imipramine/Imipramine Hydrochloride/
    Imipramine Pamoate (see p. 122)
Maprotiline Hydrochloride (see p. 140)
Nortriptyline Hydrochloride (see p. 150)
Protriptyline Hydrochloride (see p. 163)
Trimipramine Maleate (see p. 174)

Tricyclic, quadracyclic and tetracyclic antidepressants are among the most potent drugs in use today. To treat major depression, these drugs are usually given in gradually increasing doses until a distinct effect is noticed. The dosage is often lowered weeks or months later to the minimum effective dose. An antidepressant effect may begin within a few days, or only after about two weeks of therapy. Patients may be required to take maintenance doses for long periods, in order to keep depression under control.

The precise way in which these drugs work is not known, although it is believed that they may permit a normalization or an increase in the activity of nervous-system neurotransmitters within the brain that carry signals involved in causing a state of depression. Research is under way to discover the mechanisms of these effects and to create new drugs without the many possible adverse effects of the antidepressants now available.

Only your doctor can determine which (if any) antidepressant is best for you, and at what dosage level. Do not change your dosage without your doctor's approval; to do so could be extremely dangerous.

Extreme caution is required when using these drugs. Every year they are implicated in hundreds of deaths across the country, often after being used in combination with other drugs. Your doctor should be told of any other drug, whether prescription or over-the-counter, you are already taking or intend taking together with your antidepressant.

These drugs may cause serious adverse effects, even when taken exactly as prescribed. Your doctor should be notified immediately of any side effect or adverse effect you experience.

Monoamine Oxidase (MAO) Inhibitors

Isocarboxazid (see p. 125)
Phenelzine Sulfate (see p. 156)
Tranylcypromine Sulfate (see p. 166)

Monoamine oxidase (MAO) inhibitors work by slowing down the body's monoamine oxidase enzyme system which is partly responsible for regulating neurotransmitter metabolism in the body. This slowdown permits the amounts of certain naturally occurring chemicals within the body—chemicals known to affect depression—to increase.

These drugs usually require several days or weeks to take effect. Dosages must be rigidly controlled to minimize the likelihood of dangerous adverse effects occurring. In addition, many prescription and over-the-counter drugs can interact dangerously with MAO inhibitors. Check with your physician before taking any other medication.

Strict dietary restrictions must be observed while taking MAO inhibitors. Read the Cautions and Warnings for your drug very carefully. If you have any questions about which foods to avoid, consult your doctor. In addition, many prescription and over-the-counter drugs can interact dangerously with MAO inhibitors. Check with your physician before taking other medication.

Only your doctor can determine which (if any) MAO inhibitor is best for you, and at what dosage level.

Other Antidepressants

Bupropion (see p. 94)
Nomifensine Maleate (see p. 148)
Trazodone Hydrochloride (see p. 171)

Bupropion, a "second generation" antidepressant, was recently developed in the hope that it would be more effective and have fewer side effects than tricyclic and tetracyclic antidepressants. It is not known precisely how it works. Bupropion is expected to receive final FDA approval in 1985.

Nomifensine maleate, first distributed in the U.S. in 1985 after years of use in Europe, has a chemical structure somewhat different from tricyclic antidepressants, but initial tests show it has fewer side effects. It affects the neurotransmitter norepinephrine, as well as the dopamine system.

Trazodone hydrochloride, in animal studies, appears to change the way chemical messages are transmitted within the brain. It is not known precisely how it reduces depression in humans.

Only your doctor can determine whether one of these drugs should be a part of your treatment, and what dosage levels should be used.

Lithium

Lithium (see p. 133)

Lithium alters the movement of sodium in nerves and muscles and affects the way certain chemicals in the body are metabolized. It is not known exactly how it affects the manic phase of manic-depressive illness, but it is often effective within four to ten days.

Dosage levels of lithium that are considered dangerous are very close to those required for treatment. Because every person excretes lithium at a different rate, it is very important that frequent medical tests be made to determine how much lithium is in your body.

Lithium side effects and adverse effects are frequent. Consult your doctor if any occur.

Be sure to drink adequate fluids while taking lithium, and include salt in your diet.

Only your doctor can determine whether lithium should be a part of your treatment, and what dosage levels should be used.

Combination Drugs

Deprol (see p. 101)
(meprobamate and benactyzine hydrochloride)
Etrafon (see p. 113)
(perphenazine and amitriptyline hydrochloride)
Limbitrol (see p. 129)
(chlordiazepoxide and amitriptyline hydrochloride)
Triavil (see p. 174)
(perphenazine and amitriptyline hydrochloride)

These combination drugs treat anxiety and depression together. Generally, one of the ingredients is effective against anxiety, while the other is effective against depression.

Only your doctor can determine whether one of these combination drugs should be a part of your treatment, and what dosage levels should be used.

ANTIPSYCHOTICS & BETA BLOCKERS

Other drugs not profiled in this book are sometimes prescribed to treat anxiety or depression. In many cases, they do not have Food & Drug Administration (FDA) approval for these illnesses, but many doctors—relying on clinical experience—believe they may be beneficial.

Antipsychotics. These drugs are FDA approved for the treatment of such serious illnesses as psychosis and schizophrenia. Among the antipsychotics are two (chlorpromazine hydrochloride and trifluoperazine) that the FDA has approved as "possibly effective" in treating anxiety combined with neuroses. A third antipsychotic (thioridazine hydrochloride) has FDA approval for the short-term treatment of depression mixed with anxiety, although it is primarily used for serious psychotic disorders. Antipsychotics have a wide range of possible side effects and adverse effects.

Beta Blockers. These drugs are FDA approved for the treatment of high blood pressure and other illnesses of the cardiovascular system. Some of them, most frequently propranolol (Inderal), are sometimes prescribed without FDA approval to relieve the overt symptoms of anxiety or panic attacks, such as sweaty palms and muscle tension. Many doctors believe beta blockers should be given FDA approval for the treatmant of performance anxiety (stage fright) and other anxiety disorders.

Only your doctor can determine whether antipsychotics or beta blockers should be a part of your treatment and, if so, what dosage levels should be used.

DRUG PROFILES

Generic Name
Alprazolam

Brand Name

Xanax

Type of Drug

Benzodiazepine

Prescribed for

Anxiety [Under FDA review for treatment of agoraphobia with panic attacks]

Cautions and Warnings

Do not take alprazolam if you know or suspect you are sensitive or allergic to it or to any other benzodiazepine, or if you have a history of drug allergies.

Do not take alprazolam together with alcohol or other depressants.

Because alprazolam may cause drowsiness, use caution while driving, operating potentially dangerous machinery, or performing any task that requires concentration and alertness.

Alprazolam can aggravate acute narrow-angle glaucoma.

Use alprazolam with caution if you have a history of kidney or liver disease.

Alprazolam is potentially addictive and at high dosage levels can produce physical dependence in anyone. If you are predisposed to addiction, or have a family history of alcoholism, use even low doses of alprazolam with extreme caution. If you stop taking it abruptly, you may experience drug-withdrawal symptoms.

Pregnant women should avoid alprazolam, since it could cause birth defects or life-threatening withdrawal symptoms in the newborn child. It should not be used while breast-feeding.

The elderly should use small initial doses of alprazolam. Children should not use this drug.

Possible Side Effects

Tiredness and drowsiness; inability to concentrate; ataxia; gastric disturbances.

Possible Adverse Effects

Confusion; depression; lethargy; crying; headaches; inactivity; slurred speech; stupor; dizziness; tremors; change in appetite; constipation or diarrhea; dry mouth; nausea; vomiting; inability to control urination; irregular menstrual cycles; changes in heart rhythm; low blood pressure; retention of body fluids; blurred or double vision; itching; rash; hiccups; nervousness; irritability; inability to fall asleep; liver dysfunction.

Alprazolam may produce "paradoxical reactions";

while most people are calmed down by use of this drug, a small number become extremely excited, fly into rages, and experience hallucinations and increased anxiety.

Drug Interactions

Alprazolam can become extremely dangerous—even deadly—when taken together with alcohol; other tranquilizers; narcotics; anticonvulsants; sleeping pills; barbiturates; and antihistamines.

The effects of alprazolam may be stronger when taken together with cimetidine (Tagamet), which is often prescribed to treat ulcers. Alprazolam may decrease the effectiveness of the anti-Parkinson drug levodopa.

Heavy smoking may reduce the effectiveness of alprazolam.

Usual Dose

.25–4 mg. total daily, in divided doses.

Overdose

Mild alprazolam overdose causes drowsiness, mental confusion, and lethargy. Serious overdose symptoms include poor muscle coordination; low blood pressure; deep sleep; coma. If you think you are experiencing an overdose, contact your doctor or go to a hospital emergency room immediately. ALWAYS bring the medicine bottle with you.

Generic Name

Amitriptyline Hydrochloride

Brand Names

Amitril
Elavil
Emitrip
Endep
SK-Amitriptyline
(Also available in generic form)

Type of Drug

Tricyclic antidepressant

Prescribed for

Depression

Cautions and Warnings

Do not take amitriptyline hydrochloride if you know or suspect you are sensitive or allergic to it or to any other tricyclic drug.

Do not take amitriptyline hydrochloride together with alcohol or other depressant drugs.

Because amitriptyline hydrochloride may cause drowsiness, use caution while driving, operating potentially dangerous machinery, or performing any task that requires concentration and alertness.

Amitriptyline hydrochloride should not be used during the initial period of treatment for a heart attack.

Amitriptyline hydrochloride crosses the placental barrier, so it should not be used by pregnant women unless the benefits clearly outweigh the unknown potential hazards to the fetus. It should not be used while breast-feeding.

This drug should be taken with extreme caution if you have a history of convulsive disorders; have trouble urinating; have narrow angle glaucoma; suffer from heart, liver, or thyroid disease.

Abruptly stopping the use of amitriptyline hydrochloride can lead to nausea, headaches, weakness, and an over-all sense of not feeling well. Withdrawal from amitriptyline hydrochloride should take place only under a doctor's supervision. While using amitriptyline hydrochloride, do not begin or stop taking any other drug (prescription or over-the-counter) without your doctor's approval.

Notify your doctor if dry mouth, difficulty in urinating, or excessive sedation occur.

The elderly (those over 60) may become extremely confused during the initial use of amitriptyline hydrochloride. They should have regular heart exams while taking this drug. This drug is not recommended for use in children under 12 years old.

Possible Side Effects

Drowsiness; dizziness; blurred vision; dry mouth; constipation; difficulty in urinating.

Possible Adverse Effects

Changes in blood pressure; abnormal heart rate; heart attack; stroke; congestive heart failure; confusion (especially in the elderly); hallucinations; disorientation; delusions; anxiety; restlessness; excitement; numbness and tingling in the arms and legs; lack of coordination; muscle spasms or tremors; seizures and/or convulsions; skin rash; itching; ringing in the ears; retention of fluids; fever; stuffy nose; changes in composition of the blood; nausea; vomiting; loss of appetite; stomach upset; diarrhea or constipation; enlargement of the breasts in males and females; increased or decreased sex drive; irregular menstruation; swollen testicles; increased or decreased blood-sugar levels; agitation; insomnia; nightmares; feeling of panic; stomach cramps; black coloration of tongue; yellowing of eyes and/or skin; changes in liver function; weight gain or loss; sweating; flushing; need for frequent urination; drowsiness; dizziness; weakness; headaches; loss of hair.

Drug Interactions

Amitriptyline hydrochloride, if taken together with monoamine oxidase (MAO) inhibitors, can lead to a hypertensive crisis, high fevers, convulsions, and death. MAO inhibitors should not be used until at least two weeks after the last dose of amitriptyline hydrochloride.

Alcohol should be completely avoided while taking amitriptyline hydrochloride.

Amphetamines, anticoagulants (blood-thinning drugs), barbiturates and other sedatives, sleeping medications, antihypertension drugs, and thyroid medications should be used with extreme caution while taking amitriptyline hydrochloride. If amitriptyline hydrochloride is taken together with the sedative Placidyl, delirium may result.

Oral contraceptives may lessen the effects of amitriptyline hydrochloride.

Usual Dose

Initial treatment: 50 to 75 mg. total daily, in divided doses or single dose at bedtime. (Maximum 300 mg. total daily in severe cases.) Smaller doses for adolescents and the elderly.

Maintenance treatment: 50 to 150 mg. total daily,

in divided doses or single dose at bedtime. Smaller doses for adolescents and the elderly.

Overdose

Symptoms include confusion; inability to concentrate; hallucinations; drowsiness; lowered body temperature; abnormal heart rate; heart failure; enlarged eye pupils; convulsions; dangerously low blood pressure; stupor; agitation; stiffening of muscles; vomiting; high fever; coma; any of the symptoms listed under Possible Adverse Effects. Heart abnormalities caused by an overdose may recur days after other symptoms disappear, even if the overdose was small, so cardiac monitoring is required for at least 72 hours after an overdose. If you think you are experiencing an overdose, contact your doctor or go to a hospital emergency room immediately. ALWAYS bring the medicine bottle with you.

Generic Name
Amobarbital

Brand Name

Amytal

Type of Drug

Barbiturate

Prescribed for

Anxiety

Cautions and Warnings

Do not take amobarbital if you know or suspect you are sensitive or allergic to it or to any other barbiturate.

If you have ever been addicted to amobarbital, any other barbiturate, or any sedative, sleeping pills, or alcohol, you should avoid barbiturates.

Do not take amobarbital together with alcohol, antihistamines, or other depressant drugs.

Because amobarbital may cause drowsiness, use caution while driving, operating potentially dangerous machinery, or performing any task that requires concentration and alertness.

Amobarbital should be used with extreme caution if you have heart, kidney, or liver disease; breathing problems such as asthma; a history of blood disorders; hyperthyroidism.

Amobarbital should not be used by those with acute intermittent porphyria.

Notify your doctor if you experience fever; sore throat; mouth sores; easy bruising or bleeding; nose bleed.

Amobarbital is potentially addictive and at high dosage levels can produce physical dependence in anyone. If you are predisposed to addiction, or have a family history of alcoholism, use even low doses of amobarbital with extreme caution.

Pregnant women should avoid amobarbital. It should not be used while breast-feeding.

The elderly should use amobarbital with caution because it can produce confusion and can dangerously lower their body temperatures.

Possible Side Effects

Drowsiness; lethargy; skin rash; runny nose; watering eyes; itchy throat.

Possible Adverse Effects

Agitation; confusion; insomnia; anxiety; dizziness; hangover; nausea; vomiting; constipation; diarrhea; fever; headache; anemia; hyperventilation; liver damage; low blood pressure; nightmares; hallucinations; coma.

Amobarbital may produce "paradoxical reactions," especially among children and the elderly; while most people are calmed down by use of this drug, a small number become extremely excited and experience increased anxiety.

Drug Interactions

The effect of amobarbital may be increased if taken together with alcohol; narcotics; antihistamines; other barbiturates; other tranquilizers. Combining amobarbital with alcohol is especially dangerous. Monoamine oxidase (MAO) inhibitors prolong the effects of this drug.

If you take amobarbital together with anticoagulants (blood-thinning drugs), the effect of the amobarbital may be lessened.

Usual Dose

30–50 mg. two or three times daily.

Overdose

Symptoms are similar to those of an overdose of alcohol (when you drink too much): breathing slows; body temperature lowers, then elevates to fever; headache; anemia; hyperventilation; lung congestion; sleepiness. Serious overdose can lead to coma and death. If you think you are experiencing an overdose, contact your doctor or go to a hospital emergency room immediately. ALWAYS bring the medicine bottle with you.

Generic Name

Amobarbital Sodium

Brand Names

Amytal Sodium Pulvules
(Also available in generic form)

Type of Drug

Barbiturate

Prescribed for

Anxiety

Cautions and Warnings

Do not take amobarbital sodium if you know or suspect you are sensitive or allergic to it or to any other barbiturate.

If you have ever been addicted to amobarbital sodium, any other barbiturate, or any sedative, sleeping pills, or alcohol, you should avoid barbiturates.

Do not take amobarbital sodium together with alcohol, antihistamines, or other depressant drugs.

Because amobarbital sodium may cause drowsiness, use caution while driving, operating potentially dangerous machinery, or performing any task that requires concentration and alertness.

Amobarbital sodium should be used with extreme caution if you have heart, kidney, or liver disease; breathing problems such as asthma; a history of blood disorders; hyperthyroidism.

Amobarbital sodium should not be used by those with acute intermittent porphyria.

Notify your doctor if you experience fever; sore

throat; mouth sores; easy bruising or bleeding; nose bleed.

Amobarbital sodium is potentially addictive and at high dosage levels can produce physical dependence in anyone. If you are predisposed to addiction, or have a family history of alcoholism, use even low doses of this drug with extreme caution.

Pregnant women should avoid amobarbital sodium. It should not be used while breast-feeding.

The elderly should use amobarbital sodium with caution because it can produce confusion and can dangerously lower their body temperatures.

Possible Side Effects

Drowsiness; lethargy; skin rash; runny nose; watering eyes; itchy throat.

Possible Adverse Effects

Agitation; confusion; insomnia; anxiety; dizziness; hangover; nausea; vomiting; constipation; diarrhea; fever; headache; anemia; hyperventilation; liver damage; low blood pressure; nightmares; hallucinations; coma.

Amobarbital sodium may produce "paradoxical reactions," especially among children and the elderly; while most people are calmed down by use of this drug, a small number become extremely excited and experience increased anxiety.

Drug Interactions

The effect of amobarbital sodium may be increased if taken together with alcohol; narcotics; antihistamines; other barbiturates; other tranquilizers. Combining amobarbital sodium with alcohol is especially dangerous. Monoamine oxidase (MAO) inhibitors prolong the effects of this drug.

ANXIETY AND DEPRESSION

Drugs In Alphabetical Order

Adapin 10 mg **p. 110**	**Adapin** 25 mg **p. 110**	**Amitriptyline** 10 mg **p. 83**	**Amitriptyline** 25 mg **p. 83**
Amitriptyline 50 mg **p. 83**	**Amytal** 200 mg **p. 86**	**Asendin** 50 mg **p. 91**	**Atarax** 10 mg **p. 120**
Atarax 25 mg **p. 120**	**Ativan** .5 mg **p. 137**	**Ativan** 1 mg **p. 137**	**Centrax** 5 mg **p. 161**
Desyrel **p. 171**	**Elavil** 10 mg **p. 83**	**Elavil** 50 mg **p. 83**	**Elavil** 100 mg **p. 83**

A

Elavil 150 mg **p. 83**	Endep 10 mg **p. 83**	Endep 25 mg **p. 83**	Endep 50 mg **p. 83**
Endep 75 mg **p. 83**	Endep 150 mg **p. 83**	Equanil 200 mg **p. 145**	
Equanil 400 mg **p. 145**		Eskalith 300 mg **p. 133**	Etrafon 2/10 **p. 113**
Etrafon 2/25 **p. 113**	Etrafon 4/25 **p. 113**	Librium 5 mg **p. 96**	Librium 10 mg **p. 96**
Librium 25 mg **p. 96**	Limbitrol 5–12.5 **p. 129**		Limbitrol 10–25 **p. 129**

B

Ludiomil 25 mg **p. 140**	**Meprospan** 200 mg **p. 146**	**Meprospan** 400 mg **p. 146**	**Merital** 50 mg **p. 148**
Miltown **p. 146**	**Nardil** 15 mg **p. 156**	**Norpramin** 50 mg **p. 104**	**Parnate** 10 mg **p. 166**
Sinequan 10 mg **p. 110**	**Sinequan** 25 mg **p. 110**	**Sinequan** 50 mg **p. 110**	**Sinequan** 100 mg **p. 110**
SK-Lygen 5 mg **p. 96**	**SK-Lygen** 10 mg **p. 96**	**SK-Pramine** 25 mg **p. 122**	**SK-Pramine** 50 mg **p. 122**
Surmontil 25 mg **p. 174**	**Tofranil** 25 mg **p. 122**	**Tofranil** 50 mg **p. 122**	**Tofranil-PM** 75 mg **p. 122**

C

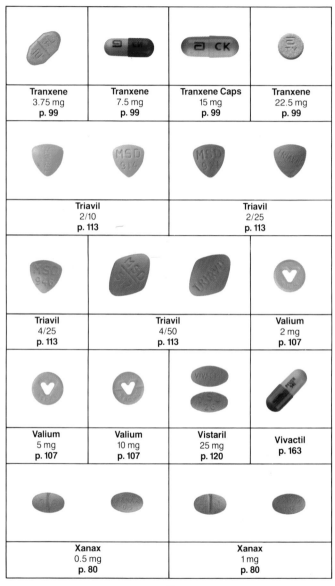

Tranxene 3.75 mg **p. 99**	**Tranxene** 7.5 mg **p. 99**	**Tranxene Caps** 15 mg **p. 99**	**Tranxene** 22.5 mg **p. 99**
Triavil 2/10 **p. 113**		**Triavil** 2/25 **p. 113**	
Triavil 4/25 **p. 113**	**Triavil** 4/50 **p. 113**		**Valium** 2 mg **p. 107**
Valium 5 mg **p. 107**	**Valium** 10 mg **p. 107**	**Vistaril** 25 mg **p. 120**	**Vivactil** **p. 163**
Xanax 0.5 mg **p. 80**		**Xanax** 1 mg **p. 80**	

D

If you take amobarbital sodium together with anticoagulants (blood-thinning drugs), the effect of the amobarbital sodium may be lessened.

Usual Dose

Individualized to suit your needs.

Overdose

Symptoms are similar to those of an overdose of alcohol (when you drink too much): breathing slows; body temperature lowers, then elevates to fever; headache; anemia; hyperventilation; lung congestion; sleepiness. Serious overdose can lead to coma and death. If you think you are experiencing an overdose, contact your doctor or go to a hospital emergency room immediately. ALWAYS bring the medicine bottle with you.

Generic Name
Amoxapine

Brand Name

Asendin

Type of Drug

Tricyclic/quadracyclic antidepressant

Prescribed for

Depression; depression mixed with anxiety

Cautions and Warnings

Do not take amoxapine if you know or suspect you are sensitive or allergic to it or to any other tricyclic drug.

Do not take amoxapine together with alcohol or other depressant drugs.

Because amoxapine may cause drowsiness, use caution while driving, operating potentially dangerous machinery, or performing any task that requires concentration and alertness.

Amoxapine should not be used during the initial period of treatment for a heart attack.

Amoxapine crosses the placental barrier, so it should not be used by pregnant women unless the benefits clearly outweigh the unknown potential hazards to the fetus. It should not be used while breast-feeding.

This drug should be taken with extreme caution if you have a history of convulsive disorders; have trouble urinating; have narrow-angle glaucoma; suffer from heart, liver, or thyroid disease.

Abruptly stopping the use of amoxapine can lead to nausea, headaches, weakness, and an over-all sense of not feeling well. Withdrawal from amoxapine should take place only under a doctor's supervision. While using amoxapine, do not begin or stop taking any other drug (prescription or over-the-counter) without your doctor's approval.

Notify your doctor if dry mouth, difficulty in urinating, or excessive sedation occur.

The elderly (those over 60) may become extremely confused during the initial use of amoxapine. They should have regular heart exams while taking this drug.

Amoxapine should not be used by children under 16.

Possible Side Effects

Drowsiness; dizziness; blurred vision; dry mouth; constipation; difficulty in urinating.

Possible Adverse Effects

Changes in blood pressure; abnormal heart rate; heart attack; stroke; congestive heart failure; confusion (especially in the elderly); hallucinations; disorientation; delusions; anxiety; restlessness; excitement; numbness and tingling in the arms and legs; lack of coordination; muscle spasms or tremors; seizures and/or convulsions; skin rash; itching; ringing in the ears; retention of fluids; fever; stuffy nose; changes in composition of the blood; nausea; vomiting; loss of appetite; stomach upset; diarrhea or constipation; enlargement of the breasts in males and females; increased or decreased sex drive; irregular menstruation; swollen testicles; increased or decreased blood-sugar levels; agitation; insomnia; nightmares; feeling of panic; stomach cramps; black coloration of tongue; yellowing of eyes and/or skin; changes in liver function; weight gain or loss; sweating; flushing; need for frequent urination; drowsiness; dizziness; weakness; headaches; loss of hair.

Drug Interactions

Amoxapine, if taken together with monoamine oxidase (MAO) inhibitors, can lead to a hypertensive crisis, or high fevers, convulsions, and death. MAO inhibitors should not be used until at least two weeks after the last dose of amoxapine.

Alcohol should be completely avoided while taking amoxapine.

Amphetamines, anticoagulants (blood-thinning drugs), barbiturates and other sedatives, sleeping medications, antihypertension drugs, and thyroid medications should be used with extreme caution while taking amoxapine. If amoxapine is taken together with the sedative Placidyl, delirium may result.

Oral contraceptives may lessen the effects of amoxapine.

Usual Dose

Initial treatment: 50 mg. three times daily. Smaller doses for the elderly.

Maintenance treatment: 100–400 mg. total daily, in divided doses or single dose at bedtime. Smaller doses for the elderly.

Overdose

Symptoms include confusion; inability to concentrate; hallucinations; drowsiness; lowered body temperature; abnormal heart rate; heart failure; enlarged eye pupils; convulsions; dangerously low blood pressure; stupor; agitation; stiffening of muscles; vomiting; high fever; coma; any of the symptoms listed under Possible Adverse Effects. Heart abnormalities caused by an overdose may recur days after other symptoms disappear, even if the overdose was small, so cardiac monitoring is required for at least 72 hours after an overdose. If you think you are experiencing an overdose, contact your doctor or go to a hospital emergency room immediately. ALWAYS bring the medicine bottle with you.

Generic Name
Bupropion

Brand Name

Wellbutrin

Type of Drug

Antidepressant

Prescribed for

Depression

Cautions and Warnings

Do not take bupropion if you know or suspect you are sensitive or allergic to it.

Because bupropion may cause dizziness, use caution while driving, operating potentially dangerous machinery, or performing any task that requires concentration and alertness.

Possible Side Effects

Weight loss; dry mouth; dizziness.

Possible Adverse Effects

Excitement; tremor; agitation; insomnia; blurred vision; constipation; nausea; vomiting; skin irritation; irregular heartbeat; headaches; sweating; seizures.

Drug Interactions

Bupropion should be used with caution with alcohol or any medication that has a depressant effect.

Usual Dose

Initial treatment: 150–600 mg. total daily.
Maintenance treatment: 150–400 mg. total daily.

Overdose

There are no known cases of bupropion overdose. Nevertheless, if you think you are experiencing an overdose, contact your doctor or go to a hospital emergency room immediately. ALWAYS take the medicine bottle with you.

Generic Name

Chlordiazepoxide Hydrochloride

Brand Name

A-poxide
Libritabs
Librium
Lipoxide
Murcil
Reposans-10
Sereen
SK-Lygen
(Also available in generic form)

Type of Drug

Benzodiazepine

Prescribed for

Anxiety

Cautions and Warnings

Do not take chlordiazepoxide hydrochloride if you know or suspect you are sensitive or allergic to it or to any other benzodiazepine, or if you have a history of drug allergies.

Do not take chlordiazepoxide hydrochloride together with alcohol or other depressants.

Because chlordiazepoxide hydrochloride may cause drowsiness, use caution while driving, operating potentially dangerous machinery, or performing any task that requires concentration and alertness.

Chlordiazepoxide hydrochloride can aggravate narrow-angle glaucoma.

Use chlordiazepoxide hydrochloride with caution if you have a history of kidney or liver disease or are undergoing anticoagulant therapy.

Chlordiazepoxide hydrochloride is potentially addictive and at high dosage levels can produce physical dependence in anyone. If you are predisposed to addiction, or have a family history of alcoholism use even low doses of chlordiazepoxide hydrochloride with extreme caution. If you stop taking it abruptly, you may experience drug-withdrawal symptoms.

Pregnant women should avoid chlordiazepoxide hydrochloride, since it could cause birth defects or life-threatening withdrawal symptoms in the newborn child. It should not be used while breastfeeding.

The elderly and children should use small initial doses of chlordiazepoxide hydrochloride.

Possible Side Effects

Tiredness and drowsiness; inability to concentrate; ataxia; gastric disturbances.

Possible Adverse Effects

Confusion; depression; lethargy; crying; headaches; inactivity; slurred speech; stupor; dizziness; tremors; change in appetite; constipation or diarrhea; dry mouth; nausea; vomiting; inability to control urination; irregular menstrual cycles; changes in heart rhythm; low blood pressure; retention of body fluids; blurred or double vision; itching; rash; hiccups; nervousness; irritability; inability to fall asleep; liver dysfunction.

Chlordiazepoxide hydrochloride may produce "paradoxical reactions"; while most people are calmed down by use of this drug, a small number become extremely excited, fly into rages, and experience hallucinations and increased anxiety.

Drug Interactions

Chlordiazepoxide hydrochloride can become extremely dangerous—even deadly—when taken together with alcohol; other tranquilizers; narcotics; anticonvulsants; sleeping pills; barbiturates; antihistamines.

The effects of chlordiazepoxide hydrochloride may be stronger when taken together with cimetidine (Tagamet), which is often prescribed to treat ulcers. Chlordiazepoxide hydrochloride may decrease the effectiveness of the anti-Parkinson drug levodopa.

Heavy smoking may reduce the effectiveness of chlordiazepoxide hydrochloride; oral contraceptives may increase its effects.

Usual Dose

5–25 mg. three to four times daily.

Overdose

Mild chlordiazepoxide hydrochloride overdose causes drowsiness, mental confusion, and lethargy. Serious overdose symptoms include poor muscle coordination; low blood pressure; deep sleep; coma. If you think you are experiencing an overdose, contact your doctor or go to a hospital emergency room immediately. ALWAYS bring the medicine bottle with you.

Generic Name

Clorazepate Dipotassium

Brand Names

Tranxene

Type of Drug

Benzodiazepine

Prescribed for

Anxiety

Cautions and Warnings

Do not take clorazepate dipotassium if you know or suspect you are sensitive or allergic to it or to any other benzodiazepine, or if you have a history of drug allergies.

Do not take clorazepate dipotassium together with alcohol or other depressants.

Because clorazepate dipotassium may cause drowsiness, use caution while driving, operating potentially dangerous machinery, or performing any task that requires concentration and alertness.

Clorazepate dipotassium can aggravate acute narrow-angle glaucoma.

Use clorazepate dipotassium with caution if you have a history of kidney or liver disease.

Clorazepate dipotassium is potentially addictive and at high dosage levels can produce physical dependence in anyone. If you are predisposed to addiction, or have a family history of alcoholism, use even low doses of clorazepate dipotassium with extreme caution. If you stop taking it abruptly, you may experience drug-withdrawal symptoms.

Pregnant women should avoid clorazepate dipotassium, since it could cause birth defects or life-threatening withdrawal symptoms in the newborn child. It should not be used while breast-feeding.

The elderly and children should use small initial doses of clorazepate dipotassium.

Possible Side Effects

Tiredness and drowsiness; inability to concentrate.

Possible Adverse Effects

Confusion; depression; lethargy; crying; headaches; inactivity; slurred speech; stupor; dizziness; tremors; change in appetite; constipation or diarrhea; dry mouth; nausea; vomiting; inability to control urination; irregular menstrual cycles; changes in heart rhythm; low blood pressure; retention of body fluids; blurred or double vision; itching; rash; hiccups; nervousness; irritability; inability to fall asleep; liver dysfunction.

Clorazepate dipotassium may produce "paradoxical reactions"; while most people are calmed down by use of this drug, a small number become extremely excited, fly into rages, and experience hallucinations and increased anxiety.

Drug Interactions

Clorazepate dipotassium can become extremely

dangerous—even deadly—when taken together with alcohol; other tranquilizers; narcotics; anticonvulsants; sleeping pills; barbiturates; and antihistamines.

The effects of clorazepate dipotassium may be stronger when taken together with cimetidine (Tagamet), which is often prescribed to treat ulcers. Clorazepate dipotassium may decrease the effectiveness of the anti-Parkinson drug levodopa.

Heavy smoking may reduce the effectiveness of clorazepate dipotassium.

Usual Dose

15–60 mg. total daily, in divided doses.

Overdose

Mild clorazepate dipotassium overdose causes drowsiness, mental confusion, and lethargy. Serious overdose symptoms include poor muscle coordination; low blood pressure; deep sleep, coma. If you think you are experiencing an overdose, contact your doctor or go to a hospital emergency room immediately. ALWAYS bring the medicine bottle with you.

Brand Name
Deprol

Ingredients

Benactyzine hydrochloride
(antidepressant)
Meprobamate
(carbamate tranquilizer)

Type of Drug

Combination

Prescribed for

Depression; depression with anxiety

Cautions and Warnings

Deprol should not be used by anyone who has shown allergic reactions to it, or to meprobamate, benactyzine hydrochloride, or related drugs.

Deprol should not be used by pregnant women or women who are breast-feeding.

Children under 6 should not use Deprol.

Deprol is potentially addictive and can at high dosage levels produce physical dependence in anyone. If you are predisposed to addiction, or have a family history of alcoholism, use even low doses of Deprol with extreme caution.

Deprol should be used with caution by those with kidney or liver problems, and by the elderly.

One of Deprol's ingredients (meprobamate) can cause seizures; it should be used with caution by epileptics.

Because Deprol may cause drowsiness, use caution while driving, operating potentially dangerous machinery, or performing any task that requires concentration and alertness.

Deprol contains tartrazine, which may cause allergic reactions especially among those allergic to aspirin.

Possible Side Effects

Drowsiness; dizziness; skin rash.

Possible Adverse Effects

Dizziness; difficulties in thinking; a sense of de-

personalization; increased anxiety; sleep disturbances; a sense of muscle relaxation; blurred
vision; dry mouth; difficulties in vision; abdominal discomfort; allergic reactions; poor muscle coordination; euphoria.

Adverse effects known to be caused by one of
Deprol's ingredients (meprobamate) include vertigo; weakness; overstimulation or excitement in
some people; nausea; vomiting; diarrhea; irregular heart rhythms; low blood pressure.

Drug Interactions

For some people, the effects of meprobamate
(one of Deprol's ingredients) may be increased by
alcohol; for others, alcohol may decrease its effects. Meprobamate's effects are likely to be stronger
if it is used together with tricyclic antidepressants
or MAO inhibitors.

Usual Dose

Initial treatment: 1 tablet three or four times
daily, gradually increased to 6 tablets maximum
daily.

Maintenance treatment: Smallest effective dose.

Overdose

Symptoms can include extreme drowsiness; lethargy; stupor; shock; failure of breathing; irregular
heartbeat; extremely low blood pressure; excessive mucus in throat and nose; coma. If you think
you are experiencing an overdose, contact your
doctor or go to a hospital emergency room immediately. ALWAYS bring the medicine bottle with
you.

Generic Name

Desipramine Hydrochloride

Brand Names

Norpramin
Pertofrane

Type of Drug

Tricyclic antidepressant

Prescribed for

Depression

Cautions and Warnings

Do not take desipramine hydrochloride if you know or suspect you are sensitive or allergic to it or to any other tricyclic drug.

Do not take desipramine hydrochloride together with alcohol or other depressant drugs.

Because desipramine hydrochloride may cause drowsiness, use caution while driving, operating potentially dangerous machinery, or performing any task that requires concentration and alertness.

Desipramine hydrochloride should not be used during the initial period of treatment for a heart attack.

Desipramine hydrochloride crosses the placental barrier, so it should not be used by pregnant women unless the benefits clearly outweigh the unknown potential hazards to the fetus. It should not be used while breast-feeding.

This drug should be taken with extreme caution if you have a history of convulsive disorders; have trouble urinating; have narrow angle glaucoma; suffer from heart, liver, or thyroid disease.

Abruptly stopping the use of desipramine hydrochloride can lead to nausea, headaches, weakness, and an over-all sense of not feeling well. Withdrawal from desipramine hydrochloride should take place under a doctor's supervision. While using desipramine hydrochloride do not begin or stop taking any other drug (prescription or over-the-counter) without your doctor's approval.

Notify your doctor if dry mouth, difficulty in urinating, or excessive sedation occur.

The elderly (those over 60), may become extremely confused during the initial use of desipramine hydrochloride. They should have regular heart exams while taking this drug.

Desipramine hydrochloride should not be used by children.

Possible Side Effects

Drowsiness; dizziness; blurred vision; dry mouth; constipation; difficulty in urinating.

Possible Adverse Effects

Changes in blood pressure; abnormal heart rates; heart attack; stroke; congestive heart failure; confusion (especially in the elderly); hallucinations; disorientation; delusions; anxiety; restlessness; excitement; numbness and tingling in the arms and legs; lack of coordination; muscle spasms or tremors; seizures and/or convulsions; skin rash; itching; ringing in the ears; retention of fluids; fever; stuffy nose; changes in composition of the blood; nausea; vomiting; loss of appetite; stomach upset; diarrhea or constipation; enlargement of the breasts in males and females; increased or decreased sex drive; irregular menstruation; swollen testicles; increased or decreased blood-sugar levels; agitation; insomnia; nightmares; feeling of panic; stomach cramps; black coloration of tongue; yellowing of eyes and/or skin; changes in liver function; weight gain or loss; sweating; flushing; need for frequent urination; drowsiness; dizziness; weakness; headaches; loss of hair.

Drug Interactions

Desipramine hydrochloride, if taken together with monoamine oxidase (MAO) inhibitors, can lead to a hypertensive crisis, or to high fever, convulsions, and death. MAO inhibitors should not be used until at least two weeks after the last dose of desipramine hydrochloride.

Alcohol should be completely avoided while taking desipramine hydrochloride.

Amphetamines, anticoagulants (blood-thinning drugs), barbiturates and other sedatives, sleeping medications, antihypertension drugs, and thyroid medications should be used with extreme caution while taking desipramine hydrochloride. If desipramine hydrochloride is taken together with the sedative Placidyl, delirium may result.

Oral contraceptives may lessen the effects of desipramine hydrochloride.

Usual Dose

Initial treatment: 75 mg. total daily, in divided doses or single dose, gradually increased to 300 mg. total daily if needed. Smaller initial doses for adolescents and the elderly.

Maintenance treatment: Smaller doses than those for initial treatment; no more than 300 mg. total daily. Smaller doses for adolescents and the elderly.

Overdose:

Symptoms include confusion; inability to concentrate; hallucinations; drowsiness; lowered body temperature; abnormal heart rate; heart failure; enlarged eye pupils; convulsions; dangerously low blood pressure; stupor; agitation; stiffening of muscles; vomiting; high fever; coma; any of the symptoms listed under Possible Adverse Effects. Heart abnormalities caused by an overdose may recur days after other symptoms disappear, even if the overdose was small, so cardiac monitoring is required for at least 72 hours after an overdose. If you think you are experiencing an overdose, contact your doctor or go to a hospital emergency room immediately. ALWAYS bring the medicine bottle with you.

Generic Name
Diazepam

Brand Names

Valium
Valrelease
(Also available in generic form)

Type of Drug

Benzodiazepine

Prescribed for

Anxiety

Cautions and Warnings

Do not take diazepam if you know or suspect you are sensitive or allergic to it or to any other benzodiazepine, or if you have a history of drug allergies.

Do not take diazepam together with alcohol or other depressants.

Because diazepam may cause drowsiness, use caution while driving, operating potentially dangerous machinery, or performing any task that requires concentration and alertness.

Diazepam can aggravate narrow-angle or open-angle glaucoma.

Use diazepam with caution if you have a history of kidney or liver disease.

Diazepam is potentially addictive and at high dosage levels can produce physical dependence in anyone. If you are predisposed to addiction, or have a family history of alcoholism, use even low doses of diazepam with extreme caution. If you stop taking it abruptly, you may experience drug-withdrawal symptoms.

Pregnant women should avoid diazepam, since it could cause birth defects or life-threatening withdrawal symptoms in the newborn child. It should not be used while breast-feeding.

The elderly and children should use small initial doses of diazepam.

Possible Side Effects

Tiredness and drowsiness; inability to concentrate; ataxia; gastric disturbances.

Possible Adverse Effects

Confusion; depression; lethargy; crying; headaches; inactivity; slurred speech; stupor; dizziness; tremors; change in appetite; constipation or diarrhea; dry mouth; nausea; vomiting; inability to control urination; irregular menstrual cycles; changes in heart rhythm; low blood pressure; retention of body fluids; blurred or double vision;

itching; rash; hiccups; nervousness; irritability; inability to fall asleep; liver dysfunction.

Diazepam may produce "paradoxical reactions"; while most people are calmed down by use of this drug, a small number become extremely excited, fly into rages, and experience hallucinations and increased anxiety.

Drug Interactions

Diazepam can become extremely dangerous—even deadly—when taken together with alcohol; other tranquilizers; narcotics; anticonvulsants; sleeping pills; barbiturates; antihistamines.

The effects of diazepam may be stronger when taken together with cimetidine (Tagamet), which is often prescribed to treat ulcers. Diazepam may decrease the effectiveness of the anti-Parkinson drug levodopa.

Heavy smoking can reduce the effectiveness of diazepam; oral contraceptives may increase its effects.

Usual Dose

2–20 mg. two to four times daily (sustained release 15–30 mg. total daily).

Overdose

Mild diazepam overdose causes drowsiness, mental confusion, and lethargy. Serious overdose symptoms include poor muscle coordination; low blood pressure; deep sleep; coma. If you think you are experiencing an overdose, contact your doctor or go to a hospital emergency room immediately. ALWAYS bring the medicine bottle with you.

Generic Name

Doxepin Hydrochloride

Brand Names

Adapin
Sinequan

Type of Drug

Tricyclic antidepressant

Prescribed for

Depression; depression mixed with anxiety; anxiety in psychoneurotic, alcoholic or organically ill patients.

Cautions and Warnings

Do not take doxepin hydrochloride if you know or suspect you are sensitive or allergic to it or to any other tricyclic drug.

Do not take doxepin hydrochloride together with alcohol or other depressant drugs.

Because doxepin hydrochloride may cause drowsiness, use caution while driving, operating potentially dangerous machinery, or performing any task that requires concentration and alertness.

Doxepin hydrochloride should not be used during the initial period of treatment for a heart attack.

Doxepin hydrochloride crosses the placental barrier, so it should not be used by pregnant women unless the benefits clearly outweigh the unknown potential hazards to the fetus. It should not be used while breast-feeding.

This drug should be taken with extreme caution if you have a history of convulsive disorders; have trouble urinating; have narrow angle glaucoma; suffer from heart, liver, or thyroid disease.

Abruptly stopping the use of doxepin hydrochloride can lead to nausea, headaches, weakness, and an over-all sense of not feeling well. Withdrawal from doxepin hydrochloride should take place only under a doctor's supervision. While using doxepin hydrochloride, do not begin or stop taking any other drug (prescription or over-the-counter) without your doctor's approval.

Notify your doctor if dry mouth, difficulty in urinating, or excessive sedation occur.

The elderly (those over 60) may become extremely confused during the initial use of doxepin hydrochloride. They should have regular heart exams while taking this drug.

Doxepin hydrochloride should not be used by children under 12.

Possible Side Effects

Drowsiness; dizziness; blurred vision; dry mouth; constipation; difficulty in urinating.

Possible Adverse Effects

Changes in blood pressure; abnormal heart rate; heart attack; stroke; congestive heart failure; confusion (especially in the elderly); hallucinations; disorientation; delusions; anxiety; restlessness; excitement; numbness and tingling in the arms and legs; lack of coordination; muscle spasms or tremors; seizures and/or convulsions; skin rash; itching; ringing in the ears; retention of fluids; fever; stuffy nose; changes in composition of the blood; nausea; vomiting; loss of appetite; stomach upset; diarrhea or constipation; enlargement of the breasts in males and females; increased or decreased sex drive; irregular menstruation; swollen testicles; increased or decreased blood-sugar levels; agitation; insomnia; nightmares; feeling of panic; stomach cramps; black coloration of tongue; yellowing of eyes and/or skin; changes in liver function; weight gain or loss; sweating; flushing; need for frequent urination; drowsiness; dizziness; weakness; headaches; loss of hair.

Drug Interactions

Doxepin hydrochloride, if taken together with monoamine oxidase (MAO) inhibitors, can lead to a hypertensive crisis, high fevers, convulsions, and death. MAO inhibitors should not be used until at least two weeks after the last dose of doxepin hydrochloride.

Alcohol should be completely avoided while taking doxepin hydrochloride.

Amphetamines, anticoagulants (blood-thinning drugs), barbiturates and other sedatives, sleeping medications, antihypertension drugs, and thyroid medications should be used with extreme caution while taking doxepin hydrochloride. If doxepin hydrochloride is taken together with the sedative Placidyl, delirium may result.

Oral contraceptives may lessen the effects of doxepin hydrochloride.

Usual Dose

Initial treatment: 25–50 mg. three times daily.

Maintenance treatment: 75–300 mg. three times daily.

While antidepressant effect may require two to three weeks of use, antianxiety effect appears rapidly.

Overdose

Symptoms include confusion; inability to concentrate; hallucinations; drowsiness; lowered body temperature; abnormal heart rate; heart failure; enlarged eye pupils; convulsions; dangerously low blood pressure; stupor; agitation; stiffening of muscles; vomiting; high fever; coma; any of the symptoms listed under Possible Adverse Effects. Heart abnormalities caused by an overdose may recur days after other symptoms disappear, even if the overdose was small, so cardiac monitoring is required for at least 72 hours after an overdose. If you think you are experiencing an overdose, contact your doctor or go to a hospital emergency room immediately. ALWAYS bring the medicine bottle with you.

Brand Names

Etrafon
Triavil

Ingredients

Amitriptyline hydrochloride
(tricyclic antidepressant)
Perphenazine
(phenothiazine antipsychotic)

Type of Drug

Combination

Prescribed for

Depression with anxiety

Cautions and Warnings

Do not take this drug if you know or suspect you are sensitive or allergic to it, to any tricyclic antidepressant, or to any phenothiazine antipsychotic. Do not use this medication together with alcohol or any other medication that produces a depressant effect.

Avoid this drug if you have any blood, liver, kidney, heart, or circulatory disease (including severely high or low blood pressure), or if you have Parkinson's disease.

Because this drug may cause drowsiness, use caution while driving, operating potentially dangerous machinery, or performing any task that requires concentration and alertness.

This drug should not be used by pregnant women unless the benefits clearly outweigh the unknown potential hazards to the fetus. It should not be used while breast-feeding.

This drug should be avoided by anyone with ulcers, narrow-angle glaucoma, convulsive disorders, or thyroid disease, or who has trouble passing urine. While using this drug, do not begin or stop taking any other medication (prescription or over-the-counter) without your doctor's approval.

Abruptly stopping the use of amitriptyline hydrochloride can lead to nausea, headaches, weakness, and an over-all sense of not feeling well. Withdrawal should take place only under a doctor's supervision.

Perphenazine, one of the ingredients in this combination drug, should not be used if you have bone-marrow depression or subcortical brain damage.

The elderly (those over 60) may become extremely confused during the initial use of amitriptyline hydrochloride. They should have regular heart exams while taking this combination drug. Additionally, the elderly are particularly sensitive to antipsychotics such as perphenazine, another component of this drug, and experience restlessness, anxiety, Parkinson's disease, and tardive dyskinesia at a relatively high rate.

Possible Side Effects

Drowsiness; dizziness; blurred vision; dry mouth; constipation; difficulty in urinating; urine may become pink or reddish brown.

Possible Adverse Effects

Amitriptyline hydrochloride one of the ingredients in this drug, may cause changes in blood pressure; abnormal heart rate; heart attack; stroke; congestive heart failure; confusion (especially in the elderly); hallucinations; disorientation; delusions; anxiety; restlessness; excitement; numbness and tingling in the arms and legs; lack of coordination; muscle spasms or tremors; seizures and/or convulsions; skin rash; itching; ringing in the ears; retention of fluids; fever; stuffy nose; changes in composition of the blood; nausea; vomiting; loss of appetite; stomach upset; diarrhea or constipation; enlargement of the breasts in males and females; increased or decreased sex drive; irregular menstruation; swollen testicles; increased or decreased blood-sugar levels; agitation; insomnia; nightmares; feeling of panic; stomach cramps; black coloration of tongue; yellowing of eyes and/or skin; changes in liver function; weight gain or loss; sweating; flushing; need for frequent urination; drowsiness; dizziness; weakness; headaches; loss of hair.

Perphenazine, one of this drug's ingredients, may

cause jaundice; changes in components of the blood; raised or lowered blood pressure; abnormal heart rate; heart attack; faintness or dizziness; tiredness; lethargy; restlessness; hyperactivity; confusion at night; bizarre dreams; inability to sleep; euphoria; breast enlargment; false-positive pregnancy tests; changes in menstrual flow; impotence and blocked ovulation; changes in sex drive; stuffy nose; headaches; nausea; vomiting; changes in appetite; changes in body temperature; loss of facial color and changes in skin color; excessive sweating and salivating; constipation; diarrhea; changes in toilet habits; blurred vision; weakening of eyelid muscles; muscle spasms; fatigue; excessive thirst.

Perphenazine (and other antipsychotics) can produce what are known as extrapyramidal effects, often associated with Parkinson's disease. Symptoms can include spasms of the neck muscles; rolling back of the eyes; convulsions; difficulty in swallowing; akathesia (restless legs). Long-term use of the drug can also cause symptoms of tardive dyskinesia, characterized by involuntary tongue movements; puffing of the cheeks; mouth puckering; chewing movements.

Drug Interactions

The use of monoamine oxidase (MAO) inhibitors together with this drug can lead to a hypertensive crisis, or to high fevers, convulsions, and death. MAO inhibitors should not be used until at least two weeks after the last dose of this drug.

Alcohol, barbiturates, sleeping pills, narcotics, and antidiarrheal medications, should be completely avoided.

Amphetamines, anticoagulants (blood-thinning drugs), antihypertension drugs, and thyroid medications should be used with extreme caution. If this drug is taken together with the sedative Placidyl, delirium may result.

Oral contraceptives may lessen the effects of amitriptyline, one of this drug's ingredients.

Usual Dose

Initial treatment: 1 tablet three or four times daily gradually increased to no more than 6 tablets total daily.

Maintenance treatment: Smallest effective dose.

Overdose

Symptoms can include confusion; extreme weakness; tiredness; inability to concentrate; hallucinations; drowsiness; lowered body temperature; abnormal heart rate; heart failure; enlarged eye pupils; dry mouth; convulsions; dangerously low blood pressure; stupor; agitation; restlessness; muscle spasms and stiffening of muscles; vomiting; high fever; coma. Heart abnormalities caused by an overdose may recur days after other symptoms disappear, even if the overdose was small, so cardiac monitoring is required for at least 72 hours after an overdose. If you think you are experiencing an overdose, contact your doctor or go to a hospital emergency room immediately. ALWAYS bring the medicine bottle with you.

Generic Name
Halazepam

Brand Name

Paxipam

Type of Drug

Benzodiazepine

Prescribed for

Anxiety

Cautions and Warnings

Do not take halazepam if you know or suspect you are sensitive or allergic to it or to any other benzodiazepine, or if you have a history of drug allergies.

Do not take halazepam together with alcohol or other depressants.

Because halazepam may cause drowsiness, use caution while driving, operating potentially dangerous machinery, or performing any task that requires concentration and alertness.

Halazepam can aggravate acute narrow-angle glaucoma.

Use halazepam with caution if you have a history of kidney or liver disease.

Halazepam is potentially addictive and at high dosage levels can produce physical dependence in anyone. If you are predisposed to addiction, or have a family history of alcoholism, use even low doses of halazepam with extreme caution. If you stop taking it abruptly, you may experience drug-withdrawal symptoms.

Pregnant women should avoid halazepam, since it could cause birth defects or life-threatening withdrawal symptoms in the newborn child. It should not be used while breast-feeding.

The elderly and children should use small initial doses of halazepam.

Possible Side Effects

Tiredness and drowsiness; inability to concentrate; ataxia; gastric disturbances.

Possible Adverse Effects

Confusion; depression; lethargy; crying; headaches; inactivity; slurred speech; stupor; dizziness; tremors; change in appetite; constipation or diarrhea; dry mouth; nausea; vomiting; inability to control urination; irregular menstrual cycles; changes in heart rhythm; low blood pressure; retention of body fluids; blurred or double vision; itching; rash; hiccups; nervousness; irritability; inability to fall asleep; liver dysfunction.

Halazepam may produce "paradoxical reactions"; while most people are calmed down by use of this drug, a small number become extremely excited, fly into rages, and experience hallucinations and increased anxiety.

Drug Interactions

Halazepam can become extremely dangerous—even deadly—when taken together with alcohol; other tranquilizers; narcotics; anticonvulsants; sleeping pills; barbiturates; antihistamines.

The effects of halazepam may be stronger when taken together with cimetidine (Tagamet), which is often prescribed to treat ulcers. Halazepam may decrease the effectiveness of the anti-Parkinson drug levodopa.

Heavy smoking may reduce the effectiveness of halazepam; oral contraceptives may increase the effect.

Usual Dose

20–40 mg. three to four times dialy.

Overdose

Mild halazepam overdose causes drowsiness, mental confusion, and lethargy. Serious overdose symptoms include poor muscle coordination; low blood pressure; deep sleep; coma. If you think you are experiencing an overdose, contact your doctor or go to a hospital emergency room immediately. ALWAYS bring the medicine bottle with you.

Generic Name

Hydroxyzine Hydrochloride/Hydroxyzine Pamoate

Brand Names

Anxanil
Atarax
Atozine
Durrax
Hy-Pam
Vamate
Vistaril
(Also available in generic form)

Type of Drug

Piperazine antihistamine

Prescribed for

Anxiety

Cautions and Warnings

Do not take hydroxyzine if you know or suspect you are sensitive or allergic to it.

Do not take hydroxyzine together with alcohol or other depressants.

Because hydroxyzine may cause drowsiness, use caution while driving, operating potentially dangerous machinery, or performing any task that requires concentration and alertness.

If you stop taking hydroxyzine abruptly, you may experience drug-withdrawal symptoms.

Pregnant women should avoid hydroxyzine. It should not be used while breast-feeding.

Possible Side Effects

Tiredness; drowsiness.

Possible Adverse Effects

Dry mouth; tremors; involuntary motor activity; convulsions; breathing difficulties.

Drug Interactions

Hydroxyzine should not be taken together with alcohol; other tranquilizers; narcotics; sleeping pills; barbiturates; monoamine oxidase (MAO) inhibitors; antipsychotics; any medication used to treat depression.

Usual Dose

50–100 mg. four times daily.

Overdose

Symptom is extreme sleepiness. If you think you are experiencing an overdose, contact your doctor or go to a hospital emergency room immediately. ALWAYS bring the medicine bottle with you.

Generic Name
Imipramine/Imipramine Hydrochloride/ Imipramine Pamoate

Brand Names

Janimine
SK-Pramine
Tipramine
Tofranil
(Also available in generic form)

Type of Drug

Tricyclic antidepressant

Prescribed for

Depression [Under FDA review for treatment of agoraphobia with panic attacks]

Cautions and Warnings

Do not take imipramine if you know or suspect you are sensitive or allergic to it or to any other tricyclic drug.

Do not take imipramine together with alcohol or other depressant drugs.

Because imipramine may cause drowsiness, use caution while driving, operating potentially dangerous machinery, or performing any task that requires concentration and alertness.

Imipramine should not be used during the initial period of treatment for a heart attack.

Imipramine crosses the placental barrier, so it should not be used by pregnant women unless the benefits clearly outweigh the unknown potential hazards to the fetus. It should not be used while breast-feeding.

This drug should be taken with extreme caution if you have a history of convulsive disorders; have trouble urinating; have narrow-angle glaucoma; suffer from heart, liver, or thyroid disease.

Abruptly stopping the use of imipramine can lead to nausea, headaches, weakness, and an overall sense of not feeling well. Withdrawal from imipramine should take place only under a doctor's supervision. While using imipramine, do not begin or stop taking any other drug (prescription or over-the-counter) without your doctor's approval.

Notify your doctor if dry mouth, difficulty in urinating or excessive sedation occur.

The elderly (those over 60) may become extremely confused during the initial use of imipramine or when taking high doses. They should have regular heart exams while taking this drug.

Tartrazine, which may cause allergic reactions especially in those allergic to aspirin, is an ingredient in Tofranil and Janimine 10 and 25 mg. tablets; Tofranil 50 mg. tablets; and Tofranil 100 and 125 mg. capsules

Possible Side Effects

Drowsiness; dizziness; blurred vision; dry mouth; constipation; difficulty in urinating.

Possible Adverse Effects

Changes in blood pressure; abnormal heart rate; heart attack; stroke; congestive heart failure; confusion (especially in the elderly); hallucinations; disorientation; delusions; anxiety; restlessness; excitement; numbness and tingling in the arms and legs; lack of coordination; muscle spasms or tremors; seizures and/or convulsions; skin rash; itching; ringing in the ears; retention of fluids; fever; stuffy nose; changes in composition of the blood; nausea; vomiting; loss of appetite; stomach upset; diarrhea or constipation; enlargement of the breasts in males and females; increased or decreased sex drive; irregular menstruation; swollen testicles; increased or decreased blood-sugar levels; agitation; insomnia; nightmares; feeling of panic; stomach cramps; black coloration of tongue; yellowing of eyes and/or skin; changes in liver function; weight gain or loss; sweating; flushing; need for frequent urination; drowsiness; dizziness; weakness; headaches; loss of hair.

Drug Interactions

Imipramine, if taken together with monoamine oxidase (MAO) inhibitors, can lead to a hypertensive crisis, high fevers, convulsions, and death. MAO inhibitors should not be used until at least two weeks after the last dose of imipramine.

Alcohol should be completely avoided while taking imipramine.

Amphetamines, anticoagulants (blood-thinning drugs), barbiturates and other sedatives, sleeping medications, antihypertension drugs, and thyroid medications should be used with extreme caution while taking imipramine. If imipramine is taken together with the sedative Placidyl, delirium may result.

Oral contraceptives may lessen the effects of imipramine.

Usual Dose

Initial treatment: 75 mg. total daily, in divided doses or single dose at bedtime, gradually increased to maximum 300 mg. total daily. Smaller doses for adolescents and the elderly.

Maintenance treatment: 50–150 mg. total daily,

in divided doses or single dose at bedtime. Smaller doses for adolescents and the elderly.

Overdose

Symptoms include confusion; inability to concentrate; hallucinations; drowsiness; lowered body temperature; abnormal heart rate; heart failure; enlarged eye pupils; convulsions; dangerously low blood pressure; stupor; agitation; stiffening of muscles; vomiting; high fever; coma; any of the symptoms listed under Possible Adverse Effects. Heart abnormalities caused by an overdose may recur days after other symptoms disappear, even if the overdose was small, so cardiac monitoring is required for at least 72 hours after an overdose. If you think you are experiencing an overdose, contact your doctor or go to a hospital emergency room immediately. ALWAYS bring the medicine bottle with you.

Generic Name
Isocarboxazid

Brand Name

Marplan

Type of Drug

Monoamine oxidase (MAO) inhibitor

Prescribed for

Depression

Cautions and Warnings

Isocarboxazid may cause a hypertensive crisis— i.e., a sudden, potentially deadly increase in blood pressure—when taken with certain foods or other medications. Symptoms of a hypertensive crisis include headache; heart palpitations; stiff or sore neck; nausea; vomiting; excessive sweating; dilated pupils; fear of bright light; irregular heart rhythm; chest pain. If any of these symptoms occur while you are taking isocarboxazid, contact your doctor or go to a hospital emergency room immediately. ALWAYS bring the medicine bottle with you.

Avoid all foods that may, in combination with MAO inhibitors, increase blood pressure. These include food products that contain tyramine, which is usually (but not always) associated with products that are aged, or that rely on putrefaction to enhance flavor. Specifically, anyone taking isocarboxazid should not eat or drink the following:

• *Cheeses*. Most cheeses, especially aged ones: blue; Boursault; natural brick; Brie; Camembert; cheddar; Emmentaler; Gruyère; mozzarella; Parmesan; Romano; Roquefort; Stilton.

• *Other dairy products.* Sour cream; yoghurt.

• *Meat/fish.* Any fish, beef, chicken liver, or other meats allowed to age without refrigeration; any meat prepared with tenderizer; any sausages (bologna, pepperoni, salami, etc.) containing aged or fermented meats; all game meats; caviar; dried fish, especially salted herring; pickled herring.

• *Alcoholic beverages.* Beer; ale; red wine, especially chianti; sherry; any undistilled beverage. It is wise to avoid all alcoholic beverages.

• *Fruits/vegetables/related foods.* Avocadoes; yeast extracts; canned figs; raisins; soy sauce.

• *Other foods.* Fava beans; large quantities of chocolate, coffee, tea, colas, and other beverages containing caffeine.

Talk with your doctor before taking any other drug whether prescription or over-the-counter. Also, over-the-counter and prescription hay fever, cold, or weight-reduction drugs should be completely avoided while using isocarboxazid.

Do not take isocarboxazid if you know or suspect you are sensitive or allergic to it or to any other MAO inhibitor.

Because isocarboxazid may cause drowsiness, use caution while driving, operating potentially dangerous machinery, or performing any task that requires concentration and alertness.

The safety of isocarboxazid during pregnancy has not been established, so it should not be used by pregnant women unless the benefits clearly outweigh the unknown potential hazards to the fetus. It should not be used while breast-feeding.

Isocarboxazid should not be used by adults over 60, or children under 16.

Isocarboxazid should not be used by anyone with a tumor known as a pheochromocytoma, or by anyone with congestive heart failure; a history of liver disease; kidney problems; cardiovascular disease; a suspected or confirmed problem involving blood supply to the brain; high blood pressure; a history of headaches.

Isocarboxazid may cause sudden drops in blood pressure when standing up, especially when the drug is first being used. If you suddenly feel dizzy upon standing, lie down until the dizziness passes.

Some isocarboxazid users experience excessive stimulation, which can usually be controlled by dosage adjustment or briefly stopping the drug under a doctor's supervision.

Isocarboxazid should be used with caution by epileptics.

Elective surgery requiring general anesthesia, and dental work using anesthesia, should be postponed until several days after the last dose of isocarboxazid.

Possible Side Effects

Dizziness; weakness; fainting; altered heart rate; vertigo; headaches; overactivity; tremors; muscle twitching; jitteriness; confusion; memory problems; insomnia; fatigue; drowsiness; restlessness; increased anxiety; nausea; diarrhea or constipation; abdominal pain; skin rash or itch; dry mouth; blurry vision; loss of appetite; weight changes; excessive sweating.

Possible Adverse Effects

Euphoria; extreme restlessness; lack of muscle coordination; tenderness; chills; palilalia (repeating words or phrases faster and faster); glaucoma; involuntary eye movements; changes in blood composition; irregular heart rhythm; painful urination; inability to control urine flow; black tongue; sensitivity to light; sexual disturbances. Rare adverse effects include convulsions; hallucinations; acute anxiety; schizophrenia; jaundice; hepatitis; blood-cell destruction; edema; ringing in the ears.

Drug Interactions

Alcoholic beverages containing tyramine should be completely avoided while taking isocarboxazid. It is wise to avoid *all* alcoholic drinks.

All drugs with stimulant properties should be avoided, including amphetamine; diet drugs; methyldopa; levodopa; dopamine, tryptophan; epinephrine; norepinephrine. Illicit stimulants, including cocaine, should be completely avoided.

Narcotics and other depressant drugs should be used with extreme caution; combining monoamine oxidase (MAO) inhibitors with depressants can lead to convulsions, coma, and death.

Isocarboxazid should not be used at the same time as any other MAO inhibitor.

Tricyclic antidepressants and related drugs should not be used together with isocarboxazid. At least 10-14 days should elapse between the last isocarboxazid dose and the first dose of any other antidepressant or MAO inhibitor.

Local anesthetics should be used cautiously during isocarboxazid treatment, as should all drugs to treat high blood pressure.

Isocarboxazid should be used cautiously together with rauwolfia drugs; guanethidine; insulin; oral sulfonylureas. This drug should not be used at the same time as any drug that tends to lower the seizure threshold, such as metrizamide.

Usual Dose

Initial treatment: 30 mg. total daily, in divided doses or single dose.

Maintenance treatment: 10–20 mg. total daily.

Overdose

Symptoms, which may not develop until 12–48 hours after overdose, include excitement; irritability; anxiety; flushing; sweating; irregular heartbeat; irregular muscle movements; exaggerated reflexes; convulsions; altered blood pressure; slowed breathing; coma. If you think you are experiencing an overdose, contact your doctor or go to a hospital emergency room immediately. ALWAYS bring the medicine bottle with you.

Brand Name
Limbitrol

Ingredients

Amitriptyline hydrochloride

(tricyclic antidepressant)
Chlordiazepoxide
(benzodiazepine)

Type of Drug

Combination

Prescribed for

Depression mixed with anxiety

Cautions and Warnings

Do not take Limbitrol if you know or suspect you are sensitive or allergic to chlordiazepoxide or any other benzodiazepine, or to amitriptyline hydrochloride or any other tricyclic antidepressant.

Limbitrol should not be used during the initial period of treatment for a heart attack.

Do not take Limbitrol together with alcohol.

Because Limbitrol may cause drowsiness, use caution while driving, operating potentially dangerous machinery, or performing any task that requires concentration and alertness.

Limbitrol should be taken with extreme caution if you have a history of convulsive disorders; have trouble urinating; have acute narrow angle glaucoma; or suffer from thyroid disease.

Abruptly stopping the use of Limbitrol can lead to nausea, headaches, weakness, and an over-all sense of not feeling well. Withdrawal from this drug should take place only under a doctor's supervision. While using Limbitrol, do not begin or stop taking any other drug, (prescription and over-the-counter) without your doctor's approval.

The elderly and children should use small initial doses of Limbitrol. Those over 60 may become extremely confused during the initial use of Limbitrol.

They should have regular heart exams while taking this drug.

Limbitrol is potentially addictive and at high dosage levels can produce physical dependence in anyone. If you are predisposed to addiction, or have a family history of alcoholism, use even low doses of Limbitrol with extreme caution.

Pregnant women should avoid Limbitrol, since it could cause birth defects or life-threatening withdrawal symptoms in the newborn child. It should not be used while breast-feeding.

Possible Side Effects

Drowsiness; dizziness; blurred vision; dry mouth; constipation; difficulty in urinating; inability to concentrate.

Possible Adverse Effects

Lethargy; disorientation; confusion (especially in the elderly); headaches; inactivity; slurred speech; stupor; dizziness; tremors; constipation; dry mouth; nausea; inability to control urination; irregular menstrual cycles; low blood pressure; retention of body fluids; blurred or double vision; itching; rash; hiccups; nervousness; liver dysfunction.

Also: changes in blood pressure; abnormal heart rates; heart attack; stroke; congestive heart failure; hallucinations; delusions; restlessness; numbness and tingling in the arms and legs; lack of coordination; muscle spasms or tremors; seizures and/or convulsions; skin rash; itching; ringing in the ears; retention of fluids; fever; stuffy nose; changes in composition of the blood; nausea; vomiting; loss of appetite; stomach upset; diarrhea or constipation; enlargement of the breasts in males and females; increased or decreased sex drive;

irregular menstruation; swollen testicles; increased or decreased blood-sugar levels; agitation; insomnia; nightmares; feeling of panic; stomach cramps; black coloration of tongue; yellowing of eyes and/or skin; changes in liver function; weight gain or loss; sweating; flushing; weakness; headaches; loss of hair.

Limbitrol may produce "paradoxical reactions"; while most people are calmed down by use of this drug, a small number become extremely excited, fly into rages, and experience hallucinations and increased anxiety.

Drug Interactions

Limbitrol can become extremely dangerous—even deadly—when taken together with alcohol; other tranquilizers; narcotics; sleeping pills; barbiturates; antihistamines.

If taken together with monoamine oxidase (MAO) inhibitors, Limbitrol can lead to a hypertensive crisis, high fevers, convulsions, and death. MAO inhibitors should not be used until at least two weeks after the last dose of Limbritrol.

Amphetamines, anticoagulants (blood-thinning drugs), antihypertension drugs, and thyroid medications should be used with extreme caution while taking Limbitrol. If Limbitrol is taken together with the sedative Placidyl, delirium may result.

Oral contraceptives may alter the effects of Limbitrol.

The effects of Limbitrol may be stronger when taken together with cimetidine (Tagamet), which is often prescribed to treat ulcers.

Heavy smoking may reduce the effectiveness of Limbitrol.

Usual Dose

Initial treatment: 1–2 tablets three or four times daily.

Maintenance treatment: Smallest effective dose.

Overdose

Symptoms include confusion; inability to concentrate; hallucinations; drowsiness; lethargy; lowered body temperature; abnormal heart rate; heart failure; enlarged eye pupils; convulsions; dangerously low blood pressure; stupor; agitation; stiffening of muscles; vomiting; high fever; deep sleep; coma. Heart abnormalities caused by an overdose may recur days after other symptoms disappear, even if the overdose was small, so cardiac monitoring is required for at least 72 hours after an overdose. If you think you are experiencing an overdose, contact your doctor or go to a hospital emergency room immediately. ALWAYS bring the medicine bottle with you.

Generic Name
Lithium

Brand Names

Eskalith
Lithane
Lithium Carbonate
Lithobid
Lithonate
Lithotabs

Type of Drug

Anti-manic

Prescribed for

Manic episodes of manic-depressive illness

Cautions and Warnings

Lithium has a relatively high incidence of side effects; prior to its use, the potential hazards should be carefully weighed against lithium's benefits. All side effects, however minor, should be promptly reported to your doctor.

Initial medical tests should be taken before lithium therapy begins; regular testing should continue throughout therapy, even if no side effects occur.

Lithium should not be used by anyone with serious kidney illness; cardiovascular disease; severe debilitation; dehydration; sodium depletion. Anyone taking diuretics, including those using diuretics to control high blood pressure, should use lithium only if carefully monitored by a physician.

Lithium should be strictly avoided by pregnant women or those contemplating becoming pregnant, because it may cause serious birth defects. This drug should not be used by women who are breast-feeding, because concentrations of lithium may appear in breast milk.

Because lithium lowers the body's ability to hold the necessary amount of salt, users should maintain an adequate diet (including salt), and drink lots of fluids—up to 10–12 glasses daily. Avoid situations that cause fluid loss, such as using a sauna. Notify your doctor if you experience frequent heavy sweating, persistent diarrhea, or develop a fever (which may be a sign of dehydration).

Lithium should be taken immediately after meals, or with food or milk.

Do not take lithium if you know or suspect you are sensitive or allergic to it.

Children under 12 should not use lithium.

Because lithium may cause drowsiness, use caution while driving, operating potentially dangerous machinery, or performing any task that requires concentration and alertness.

Lithane tablets contain tartrazine, which may cause allergic reactions especially in those allergic to aspirin.

An identification/instruction card (Medic Alert) should be carried in wallet or purse, listing your ailment, the medications and doses you're taking, and the name and phone number of your doctor.

Possible Side Effects and Adverse Effects

Side effects and adverse effects are common enough to be generally indistinguishable. While some can occur regardless of dosage levels, many are related to the amount of lithium in the body. Because the drug is excreted at a different rate by each user—and levels in the body can therefore vary widely regardless of dosage—these side effects may or may not be tied to the amount of lithium taken. Side effects and adverse effects can include:

Headache; fever; short-term memory impairment; hand tremors; nausea; general discomfort; vomiting; diarrhea; thirst; excess salivation; dry mouth; stomach upset; loss of appetite; stomach gas; indigestion; abdominal pain; drowsiness; lethargy; confusion; restlessness; dizziness; blurred vision; slurred speech; ringing in the ears; giddiness; muscle weakness and/or pain; twitching; irregular tongue movements; loss of coordination; fainting; blackouts; changes in taste perception (salty taste); swollen lips; tooth cavities; loss of hair; drying of hair.

Also: increased urinary output; inability to control urination or bowel movements; skin irritation;

rash; acne and acnelike irritations; loss of feeling in skin; skin ulcers; swelling of ankles and wrists; swollen and painful joints; weight gain or loss; tightness in chest; eye irritation; visual disturbances; hallucinations; worsening of cataracts; seizures; stupor; severe low blood pressure; impotence or reductions in sexual ability; changes in brainwaves, heartbeat, blood composition and thyroid activity; goiter; worsening of existing organic brain syndrome; irreversible diabetes; respiratory failure; changes in heart rhythm.

Death can occur from lithium regardless of the dosage, usually as the result of lithium-related breathing problems.

Drug Interactions

Drugs that reduce the acidity of urine (including antacids) as well as some diuretic drugs (osmotic diuretics and theophyllines) lower the amount of lithium in the body and reduce its beneficial effects.

Doses of thiazide diuretics and lithium may have to be altered if used together. Potassium-sparing diuretics should be used with great caution.

Ethacrynic acid and furosemide should be used with caution together with lithium.

Nonsteroidal anti-inflammatory drugs, including indomethacin, should be used with lithium only if more-frequent medical tests are made.

Drugs believed to increase levels of lithium in the body, and possibly to lead to toxic overdoses, include mazindol, tetracycline, phenytoin, methyldopa, and carbamazepine.

The antipsychotic drug haloperidol when combined with lithium has been associated with severe side effects, including brain damage, but no firm cause-and-effect relationship has been established. Nevertheless, haloperidol and other antipsychotics should be used with caution.

Phenothiazine and neuromuscular blocking drugs, as well as sympathomimetic amines and iodide salts, should also be used with caution together with lithium.

Usual Dose

Initial treatment: 300 mg. two or three times daily.
Maintenance treatment: Individualized according to lithium levels in the body, as determined by medical tests; usually 300 mg. three to four times daily. Maximum 3600 mg. total daily.

Overdose

Because lithium's toxic overdose levels are so close to dosages used to treat manic-depressive disorders, overdose symptoms can include any number of the symptoms listed above under Possible Side Effects and Adverse Effects. When serious side effects occur soon after treatment begins, or when any side effects occur later during lithium treatment, inform your doctor immediately. If you think you are experiencing an overdose, contact your doctor to go to a hospital emergency room immediately. ALWAYS bring the medicine bottle with you.

Generic Name
Lorazepam

Brand Name

Ativan

Type of Drug

Benzodiazepine

Prescribed for

Anxiety

Cautions and Warnings

Do not take lorazepam if you know or suspect you are sensitive or allergic to it or to any other benzodiazepine, or if you have a history of drug allergies.

Do not take lorazepam together with alcohol or other depressants.

Because lorazepam may cause drowsiness, use caution while driving, operating potentially dangerous machinery, or performing any task that requires concentration and alertness.

Lorazepam can aggravate acute narrow-angle glaucoma.

Use lorazepam with caution if you have a history of kidney or liver disease.

Lorazepam is potentially addictive and at high dosage levels can produce physical dependence in anyone. If you are predisposed to addiction, or have a family history of alcoholism, use even low doses of lorazepam with extreme caution. If you stop taking it abruptly, you may experience drug-withdrawal symptoms.

Pregnant women should avoid lorazepam, since it could cause birth defects or life-threatening withdrawal symptoms in the newborn child. It should not be used while breast-feeding.

The elderly and children should use small initial doses of lorazepam.

Possible Side Effects

Tiredness and drowsiness; inability to concentrate; ataxia; gastric disturbances.

Possible Adverse Effects

Confusion; depression; lethargy; crying; headaches; inactivity; slurred speech; stupor; dizziness; tremors; change in appetite; constipation or diarrhea; dry mouth; nausea; vomiting; inability to control urination; irregular menstrual cycles; changes in heart rhythm; low or high blood pressure; retention of body fluids; blurred or double vision; itching; rash; hiccups; nervousness; irritability; inability to fall asleep; liver dysfunction.

Lorazepam may produce "paradoxical reactions"; while most people are calmed down by use of this drug, a small number become extremely excited, fly into rages, and experience hallucinations and increased anxiety.

Drug Interactions

Lorazepam can become extremely dangerous— even deadly—when taken together with alcohol; other tranquilizers; narcotics; anticonvulsants; sleeping pills; barbiturates; and antihistamines.

Lorazepam may decrease the effectiveness of the anti-Parkinson drug levodopa.

Heavy smoking may reduce the effectiveness of lorazepam.

Usual Dose

2–10 mg. total daily, in divided doses.

Overdose

Mild lorazepam overdose causes drowsiness, mental confusion, and lethargy. Serious overdose symptoms include poor muscle coordination; low blood pressure; deep sleep; coma. If you think you are experiencing an overdose, contact your doctor or go to a hospital emergency room immediately. ALWAYS bring the medicine bottle with you.

Generic Name
Maprotiline Hydrochloride

Brand Name

Ludiomil

Type of Drug

Tetracyclic antidepressant

Prescribed for

Depression; anxiety associated with depression

Cautions and Warnings

Do not take maprotiline hydrochloride if you know or suspect you are sensitive or allergic to it or to any other tricyclic or tetracyclic drug.

Maprotiline hydrochloride should not be used during the initial period of treatment for a heart attack.

Because maprotiline hydrochloride may cause drowsiness, use caution while driving, operating potentially dangerous machinery, or performing any task that requires concentration and alertness.

Maprotiline hydrochloride crosses the placental barrier, so it should not be used by pregnant women unless the benefits clearly outweigh the unknown potential hazards to the fetus. It should not be used while breast-feeding.

This drug should be taken with extreme caution if you have a history of seizures or convulsive disorders; have trouble urinating; have narrow angle glaucoma; suffer from heart, liver, or thyroid disease.

Abruptly stopping the use of maprotiline hydrochloride can lead to nausea, headaches, weakness, and an over-all sense of not feeling well. Withdrawal from maprotiline hydrochloride should take place only under a doctor's supervision. While using maprotiline hydrochloride, do not begin or stop taking any other drug (prescription or over-the-counter) without your doctor's approval.

Notify your doctor if extreme dry mouth, difficulty in urinating or excessive sedation occur.

The elderly (those over 60) may become extremely confused during the initial use of maprotiline hydrochloride. They should have regular heart exams while taking this drug.

Maprotiline hydrochloride should not be used by anyone under 18.

Possible Side Effects

Drowsiness; dizziness; blurred vision; dry mouth; constipation; difficulty in urinating.

Possible Adverse Effects

Changes in blood pressure; abnormal heart rate; heart attack; stroke; congestive heart failure; confusion (especially in the elderly); hallucinations; disorientation; delusions; anxiety; restlessness; excitement; numbness and tingling in the arms and legs; lack of coordination; muscles spasms or tremors; seizures and/or convulsions; skin rash; itching; ringing in the ears; retention of fluids; fever; stuffy nose; changes in composition of the blood; nausea; vomiting; loss of appetite; stomach upset; diarrhea or constipation; enlargement of the breasts in males and females; increased or decreased sex drive; irregular menstruation; swollen testicles; increased or decreased blood-sugar levels; agitation; insomnia; nightmares; feeling of panic; stomach cramps; black coloration of tongue; yellowing of eyes and/or skin; changes in liver function; weight gain or loss; sweating; flushing; need for frequent urination; drowsiness; dizziness; weakness; headaches; loss of hair.

Drug Interactions

Maprotiline hydrochloride, if taken together with monoamine oxidase (MAO) inhibitors, can lead to a hypertensive crisis, high fevers, convulsions, and death. MAO inhibitors should not be used until at least two weeks after the last dose of maprotiline hydrochloride.

Alcohol should be completely avoided while taking maprotiline hydrochloride.

Amphetamines, anticoagulants (blood-thinning drugs), barbiturates and other sedatives, sleeping medications, antihypertension drugs, and thyroid medications should be used with extreme caution while taking maprotiline hydrochloride. If maprotiline hydrochloride is taken together with the sedative Placidyl, delirium may result.

Oral contraceptives may lessen the effects of maprotiline hydrochloride.

Usual Dose

Initial treatment: 75 mg. total daily for two weeks, increased to maximum 225 mg. daily for additional six weeks. Smaller doses for the elderly.

Maintenance treatment: 50–200 mg. total daily (usually 75–150 mg. total daily). Smaller doses for the elderly.

Overdose

Symptoms include confusion; inability to concentrate; hallucinations; drowsiness; lowered body temperature; abnormal heart rate; heart failure; enlarged eye pupils; convulsions; dangerously low blood pressure; stupor; agitation; stiffening of muscles; vomiting; high fever; coma; any of the symptoms listed under Possible Adverse Effects. Heart abnormalities caused by an overdose may recur days after other symptoms disappear, even if the overdose was small, so cardiac monitoring is required for at least 72 hours after an overdose. If you think you are experiencing an overdose, contact your doctor or go to a hospital emergency room immediately. ALWAYS bring the medicine bottle with you.

Generic Name
Mephobarbital

Brand Name

Mebaral

Type of Drug

Barbiturate

Prescribed for

Anxiety

Cautions and Warnings

Do not take mephobarbital if you know or suspect you are sensitive or allergic to it or to any other barbiturate.

If you have ever been addicted to mephobarbital, any other barbiturate, or any sedative, sleeping pills, or alcohol, you should avoid barbiturates.

Do not take mephobarbital together with alcohol, antihistamines, or other depressant drugs.

Because mephobarbital may cause drowsiness, use caution while driving, operating potentially dangerous machinery, or performing any task that requires concentration and alertness.

Mephobarbital should be used with extreme caution if you have heart, kidney, or liver disease; breathing problems such as asthma; a history of blood disorders; hyperthyroidism.

Mephobarbital should not be used by those with acute intermittent porphyria.

Notify your doctor if you experience fever; sore throat; mouth sores; easy bruising or bleeding; nose bleed.

Mephobarbital is potentially addictive and at high dosage levels can produce physical dependence in anyone. If you are predisposed to addiction, or have a family history of alcoholism, use even low doses of this drug with extreme caution.

Pregnant women should avoid mephobarbital. It should not be used while breast-feeding.

The elderly should use mephobarbital with caution because it can produce confusion and can dangerously lower their body temperatures.

Possible Side Effects

Drowsiness; lethargy; skin rash; runny nose; watering eyes; itchy throat.

Possible Adverse Effects

Agitation; confusion; insomnia; anxiety; dizziness; hangover; nausea; vomiting; constipation; diarrhea; fever; headache; anemia; hyperventilation; liver damage; low blood pressure; nightmares; hallucinations; coma.

Mephobarbital may produce "paradoxical reactions," especially among children and the elderly; while most people are calmed down by use of this drug, a small number become extremely excited and experience increased anxiety.

Drug Interactions

The effect of mephobarbital may be increased if taken together with alcohol; narcotics; antihistamines; other barbiturates; other tranquilizers. Combining this drug with alcohol is especially dangerous. Monoamine oxidase (MAO) inhibitors prolong the effects of this drug.

If you take mephobarbital together with anticoagulants (blood-thinning drugs), the effect of the mephobarbital may be lessened.

Usual Dose

32–100 mg. three or four times daily.

Overdose

Symptoms are similar to those of an overdose of alcohol (when you drink too much): breathing slows; body temperature lowers, then elevates to fever; headache; anemia; hyperventilation; lung congestion; sleepiness. Serious overdose can lead to coma and death. If you think you are experiencing an overdose, contact your doctor or go to a hospital emergency room immediately. ALWAYS bring the medicine bottle with you.

Generic Name:
Meprobamate

Brand Names:

Equanil

Equanil Tablets and Wyseals
Mepriam
Meprospan
Miltown
Neuramate
Neurate-400
Sedabamate
SK-Bamate
Tranmep
(also available in generic form)

Type of Drug

Carbamate tranquilizer

Prescribed for

Anxiety

Cautions and Warnings

Do not take meprobamate if you know or suspect you are sensitive or allergic to it or to any related drug.

Do not take meprobamate together with alcohol or other depressants.

Because meprobamate may cause drowsiness, use caution while driving, operating potentially dangerous machinery, or performing any task that requires concentration and alertness.

Meprobamate should not be used by pregnant women or women who are breast-feeding. It should not be used by children under age 6.

Meprobamate is potentially addictive. If you are predisposed to addiction, or have a family history of alcoholism, use meprobamate with extreme caution. If you stop taking it abruptly, you may experience drug-withdrawal symptoms.

Meprobamate should be used with caution by

those with kidney or liver problems, and by the elderly.

Meprobamate should not be used by those with acute intermittent porphyria.

Because meprobamate can cause seizures, it should be used with caution by epileptics.

Equanil Wyseals contain tartrazine, which may cause allergic reactions especially among those allergic to aspirin.

Possible Side Effects

Drowsiness; dizziness; blurred vision; skin rash; sore throat; fever.

Possible Adverse Effects

Slurred speech; ataxia; headaches; vertigo; weakness; overstimulation or excitement in some people; nausea; vomiting; diarrhea; irregular heart rhythms; low blood pressure; itching; serious allergic reactions.

Drug Interactions

For some people, alcohol may increase the effects of meprobamate; for others, alcohol may decrease its effects. Alcohol should be completely avoided while taking meprobamate.

Meprobamate's effects are likely to be stronger if used together with tricyclic antidepressants, MAO inhibitors, or other depressants.

Usual Dose

Adults: 1,200–2,400 mg. total daily, divided into three to four doses; smaller doses for children

Overdose

Symptoms can include extreme drowsiness; lethargy; stupor; shock; failure of breathing; irregular heartbeat; extremely low blood pressure; excessive mucus in throat and nose; coma. If you think you are experiencing an overdose, contact your doctor or go to a hospital emergency room immediately. ALWAYS bring the medicine bottle with you.

Generic Name
Nomifensine Maleate

Brand Name

Merital

Type of Drug

Tetrahydroisoquinoline antidepressant

Prescribed for

Depression

Cautions and Warnings

Do not take nomifensine maleate if you know, or suspect, your are sensitive or allergic to it.

Do not take nomifensine maleate together with alcohol.

Because nomifensine maleate may impair mental and physical ability, use caution while driving, operating potentially dangerous machinery, or performing any task that requires concentration and alertness until you are certain the drug is not affecting you adversely.

Nomifensine maleate should not be used by pregnant women unless the potential benefits clearly outweigh the potential unknown hazards to the fetus. It should be used with caution while breast feeding.

While using nomifensine maleate, avoid cold remedies, decongestants, and local anesthetics.

Nomifensine maleate should be taken cautiously by anyone recovering from a heart attack; who has serious liver or kidney illness; or who has a serious blood disorder.

Nomifensine maleate may produce fever, or increase a fever already present. Notify your doctor immediately if this occurs.

This drug should not be used by children under 18.

Nomifensine maleate should not be taken with food, or within an hour after eating. It should not be taken after the mid-afternoon, because it may cause insomnia.

Since nomifensine maleate acts as a stimulant in some people, it should be used cautiously by those with a history of abusing stimulants such as amphetamine.

Possible Side Effects

Dry mouth; bad taste; nervousness; restlessness; insomnia; sleep disturbances; nausea; vomiting; constipation.

Possible Adverse Effects

Fever; anemia; liver or kidney damage; headaches; dizziness; trembling; blurred vision; diarrhea; stomach upset; skin irritation; general aches and pains; loss of appetite; hot flashes.

Drug Interactions

Nomifensine maleate should not be taken together with monoamine oxidase (MAO) inhibitors;

there should be a two-week period between the use of MAO inhibitors and this drug.

Alcohol should be strictly avoided while taking nomifensine maleate.

Avoid cold remedies, decongestants and local anesthetics while taking nomifensine maleate.

Nomifensine maleate should be taken cautiously with drugs used to treat high blood pressure.

Usual Dose

Initial Treatment: 100 mg. total daily in two equally divided doses, gradually increased to maximum 200 mg. total daily. Smaller doses for the elderly.

Maintenance treatment: Smallest effective dose.

Overdose

Symptoms include drowsiness; tremor; irregular heart rhythm; high blood pressure; larger or smaller eye pupils; and coma. If you think you are experiencing an overdose, contact your doctor or go to a hospital emergency room immediately. ALWAYS bring the medicine bottle with you.

Generic Name:
Nortriptyline Hydrochloride

Brand Names

Aventyl Hydrochloride
Pamelor

Type of Drug

Tricyclic antidepressant

Prescribed for

Depression; depression mixed with anxiety

Cautions and Warnings

Do not take nortriptyline hydrochloride if you know or suspect you are sensitive or allergic to it or to any other tricyclic drug.

Do not take nortriptyline hydrochloride together with alcohol or other depressant drugs.

Because nortriptyline hydrochloride may cause drowsiness, use caution while driving, operating potentially dangerous machinery, or performing any task that requires concentration and alertness.

Nortriptyline hydrochloride should not be used during the initial period of treatment for a heart attack.

Nortriptyline hydrochloride crosses the placental barrier, so it should not be used by pregnant women unless the benefits clearly outweigh the unknown potential hazards to the fetus. It should not be used while breast-feeding.

This drug should be taken with extreme caution if you have a history of convulsive disorders; have trouble urinating; have glaucoma; suffer from heart, liver, or thyroid disease.

Abruptly stopping the use of nortriptyline hydrochloride can lead to nausea, headaches, weakness, and an over-all sense of not feeling well. Withdrawal from nortriptyline hydrochloride should take place only under a doctor's supervision. While using nortriptyline hydrochloride, do not begin or stop taking any other drug (prescription or over-the-counter) without your doctor's approval.

Notify your doctor if dry mouth, difficulty in urination, or excessive sedation occur.

The elderly (those over 60) may become extremely confused during the initial use of nortriptyline hydrochloride. They should have regular heart exams while taking this drug.

Nortriptyline hydrochloride should not be used by children.

Possible Side Effects

Drowsiness; dizziness; blurred vision; dry mouth; constipation; difficulty in urinating.

Possible Adverse Effects

Changes in blood pressure; abnormal heart rate; heart attack; stroke; congestive heart failure; confusion (especially in the elderly); hallucinations; disorientation; delusions; anxiety; restlessness; excitement; numbness and tingling in the arms and legs; lack of coordination; muscle spasms or tremors; seizures and/or convulsions; skin rash; itching; ringing in the ears; retention of fluids; fever; stuffy nose; changes in composition of the blood; nausea; vomiting; loss of appetite; stomach upset; diarrhea or constipation; enlargement of the breasts in males and females; increased or decreased sex drive; irregular menstruation; swollen testicles; increased or decreased blood-sugar levels; agitation; insomnia; nightmares; feeling of panic; stomach cramps; black coloration of tongue; yellowing of eyes and/or skin; changes in liver function; weight gain or loss; sweating; flushing; need for frequent urination; drowsiness; dizziness; weakness; headaches; loss of hair.

Drug Interactions

Nortriptyline hydrochloride, if taken together with monoamine oxidase (MAO) inhibitors, can lead to a hypertensive crisis, or to high fevers, convulsions, and death. MAO inhibitors should not be used until at least two weeks after the last dose of nortriptyline hydrochloride.

Alcohol should be completely avoided while taking nortriptyline hydrochloride.

Amphetamines, anticoagulants (blood-thinning drugs), barbiturates and other sedatives, sleeping medications, antihypertension drugs, and thyroid medications should be used with extreme caution while taking nortriptyline hydrochloride. If nortriptyline hydrochloride is taken together with the sedative Placidyl, delirium may result.

Oral contraceptives may lessen the effects of nortriptyline hydrochloride.

Usual Dose

25 mg. three to four times daily. Lower doses for adolescents and the elderly.

Overdose

Symptoms include confusion; inability to concentrate: hallucinations; drowsiness; lowered body temperature; abnormal heart rate; heart failure; enlarged eye pupils; convulsions; dangerously low blood pressure; stupor; agitation; stiffening of muscles; vomiting; high fever; coma; any of the symptoms listed under Possible Adverse Effects. Heart abnormalities caused by an overdose may recur days after other symptoms disappear, even if the overdose was small, so cardiac monitoring is required for at least 72 hours after an overdose. If you think you are experiencing an overdose, contact your doctor or go to a hospital emergency room immediately. ALWAYS bring the medicine bottle with you.

Generic Name

Oxazepam

Brand Name

Serax

Type of Drug

Benzodiazepine

Prescribed for

Anxiety

Cautions and Warnings

Do not take oxazepam if you know or suspect you are sensitive or allergic to it or to any other benzodiazepine, or if you have a history of drug allergies.

Do not take oxazepam together with alcohol or other depressants.

Because oxazepam may cause drowsiness, use caution while driving, operating potentially dangerous machinery, or performing any task that requires concentration and alertness.

Oxazepam can aggrevate acute narrow-angle glaucoma.

Use oxazepam with caution if you have a history of kidney or liver disease.

Oxazepam is potentially addictive and at high dosage levels can produce physical dependence in anyone. If you are predisposed to addiction, or have a family history of alcoholism, use even low doses of oxazepam with extreme caution. If you stop taking it abruptly, you may experience drug-withdrawal symptoms.

Pregnant women should avoid oxazepam, since it could cause birth defects or life-threatening withdrawal symptoms in the newborn child. It should not be used while breast-feeding.

The elderly and children should use small initial doses of oxazepam.

Serax 15 mg. tablets contain tartrazine, which may cause allergic reactions especially among those allergic to aspirin.

Possible Side Effects

Tiredness and drowsiness; inability to concentrate; ataxia; gastric disturbances.

Possible Adverse Effects

Confusion; depression; lethargy; crying; headaches; inactivity; slurred speech; stupor; dizziness; tremors; change in appetite; constipation or diarrhea; dry mouth; nausea; vomiting; inability to control urination; irregular menstrual cycles; changes in heart rhythm; low blood pressure; retention of body fluids; blurred or double vision; itching; rash; hiccups; nervousness; irritability; inability to fall asleep; liver dysfunction.

Oxazepam may produce "paradoxical reactions"; while most people are calmed down by use of this drug, a small number become extremely excited, fly into rages, and experience hallucinations and increased anxiety.

Drug Interactions

Oxazepam can become extremely dangerous— even deadly—when taken together with alcohol; other tranquilizers; narcotics; anticonvulsants; sleeping pills; barbiturates; and antihistamines.

Oxazepam may decrease the effectivness of the anti-Parkinson drug levodopa.

Heavy smoking may reduce the effectiveness of oxazepam.

Usual Dose

10–30 mg. three or four times daily.

Overdose

Mild oxazepam overdose causes drowsiness, mental confusion, and lethargy. Serious overdose symptoms include poor muscle coordination; low blood pressure; deep sleep; coma. If you think you are experiencing an overdose, contact your doctor or go to a hospital emergency room immediately. ALWAYS bring the medicine bottle with you.

Generic Name
Phenelzine Sulfate

Brand Name

Nardil

Type of Drug

Monoamine oxidase (MAO) inhibitor

Prescribed for

Depression [Under FDA review for treatment of agoraphobia with panic attacks]

Cautions and Warnings

Phenelzine sulfate may cause a hypertensive crisis—i.e., a sudden, potentially deadly increase in blood pressure—when taken with certain foods or other medications. Symptoms of a hypertensive crisis include headache; heart palpitations; stiff or sore neck; nausea; vomiting; excessive sweating; dilated pupils; fear of bright light; irregular heart rhythms; chest pain. If any of these symptoms occur while you are taking phenelzine sulfate, contact your doctor or visit a hospital emergency room immediately. ALWAYS bring the medicine bottle with you.

Avoid all foods that may, in combination with MAO inhibitors, increase blood pressure. These include food products that contain tyramine, which is usually (but not always) associated with products that are aged, or that rely on putrefaction to enhance flavor. Specifically, anyone taking phenelzine sulfate should not eat or drink the following:

• *Cheeses.* Most cheeses, especially aged ones: blue; Boursault; natural brick; Brie; Camembert; cheddar; Emmentaler; Gruyère; mozzarella; Parmesan; Romano; Roquefort; Stilton.
• *Other dairy products.* Sour cream; yoghurt.
• *Meat Fish.* Any fish, beef, chicken liver, or other meats allowed to age without refrigeration; any meat prepared with tenderizer; any sausages (bologna, pepperoni, salami, etc.) containing aged or fermented meats; all game meats; caviar; dried fish, especially salted herring; pickled herring.
• *Alcoholic beverages.* Beer; ale; red wine, especially chianti; sherry; any undistilled beverage. It is wise to avoid all alcoholic beverages.
• *Fruits/vegetables/related foods.* Avocadoes; yeast extracts; bananas; canned figs; raisins; soy sauce.
• *Other foods:* Fava beans; large quantities of chocolate, coffee, tea, colas, and other beverages containing caffeine.

*　　*　　*

Talk with your doctor before taking any other drug whether prescription or over-the-counter. Also, over-the-counter and prescription hay fever, cold, or weight-reduction drugs should be completely avoided while using phenelzine sulfate.

Do not take phenelzine sulfate if you know or suspect you are sensitive or allergic to it or to any other MAO inhibitor.

Because phenelzine sulfate may cause drowsiness, use caution while driving, operating potentially dangerous machinery, or performing any task that requires concentration and alertness.

The safety of phenelzine sulfate during pregnancy has not been established, so it should not be used by pregnant women unless the benefits clearly outweigh the unknown potential hazards to the fetus. It should not be used while breast-feeding.

Phenelzine sulfate should not be used by adults over 60, or children under 16.

Phenelzine sulfate should not be used by anyone with a tumor known as a pheochromocytoma, or by anyone with congestive heart failure; a history of liver disease; kidney problems; cardiovascular disease; a suspected or confirmed problem involving blood supply to the brain; high blood pressure; a history of headaches.

Phenelzine sulfate may cause sudden drops in blood pressure when standing up, especially when the drug is first being used. If you suddenly feel dizzy upon standing, lie down until the dizziness passes.

Some phenelzine sulfate users experience excessive stimulation, which can usually be controlled by dosage adjustment or briefly stopping the drug under a doctor's supervision.

Phenelzine sulfate should be used with caution by epileptics.

Elective surgery requiring general anesthesia, and

dental work using anesthesia, should be postponed until several days after the last dose of phenelzine sulfate.

Possible Side Effects

Dizziness; weakness; fainting; altered heart rate; vertigo; headaches; overactivity; tremors; muscle twitching; jitteriness; confusion; memory problems; insomnia; fatigue; drowsiness; restlessness; increased anxiety; nausea; diarrhea or constipation; abdominal pain; skin rash or itch; dry mouth; blurry vision; loss of appetite; weight changes; excessive sweating.

Possible Adverse Effects

Euphoria; extreme restlessness; lack of muscle coordination; tenderness; chills; palilalia (repeating words or phrases faster and faster); glaucoma; involuntary eye movements; changes in blood composition; irregular heart rhythm; painful urination; inability to control urine flow; black tongue; sensitivity to light; sexual disturbances. Rare adverse effects include convulsions; hallucinations; acute anxiety; schizophrenia; jaundice; hepatitis; blood-cell destruction; edema; ringing in the ears.

Drug Interactions

Alcoholic beverages containing tyramine should be completely avoided while taking phenelzine sulfate. It is wise to avoid *all* alcoholic drinks.

All drugs with stimulant properties should be avoided, including amphetamine; diet drugs; methyldopa; levodopa; dopamine; tryptophan; epinephrine; norepinephrine. Illicit stimulants, including cocaine, should be completely avoided.

Narcotics and other depressant drugs should be

used with extreme caution; combining monoamine oxidase (MAO) inhibitors with depressants can lead to convulsions, coma, and death.

Phenelzine sulfate should not be used at the same time as any other MAO inhibitor.

Tricyclic antidepressants and related drugs should not be used together with phenelzine sulfate. At least ten days should elapse between the last phenelzine sulfate dose and the first dose of any other antidepressant or MAO inhibitor.

All drugs to treat high blood pressure should be used cautiously during phenelzine sulfate treatment.

Phenelzine sulfate should be used cautiously together with rauwolfia drugs; guanethidine; insulin; oral sulfonylureas. This drug should not be used at the same time as any drug that tends to lower the seizure threshold, such as metrizamide.

Usual Dose

Initial treatment: 15 mg. three times daily, quickly increased to 60–90 mg. total daily.

Maintenance treatment: 15 mg. or more total daily, or every other day, depending on individual response.

Overdose

Symptoms, which may not develop until 12–48 hours after overdose, include excitement; irritability; anxiety; flushing; sweating; irregular heartbeat; irregular muscle movements; exaggerated reflexes; convulsions; altered blood pressure; slowed breathing; coma. If you think you are experiencing an overdose, contact your doctor or go to a hospital emergency room immediately. ALWAYS bring the medicine bottle with you.

Generic Name

Prazepam

Brand Name

Centrax

Type of Drug

Benzodiazepine

Prescribed for

Anxiety

Cautions and Warnings

Do not take prazepam if you know or suspect you are sensitive or allergic to it or to any other benzodiazepine, or if you have a history of drug allergies.

Do not take prazepam together with alcohol or other depressants.

Because prazepam may cause drowsiness, use caution while driving, operating potentially dangerous machinery, or performing any task that requires concentration and alertness.

Prazepam can aggravate acute narrow-angle glaucoma.

Use prazepam with caution if you have a history of kidney or liver disease.

Prazepam is potentially addictive and at high dosage levels can produce physical dependence in anyone. If you are predisposed to addiction, or have a family history of alcoholism, use even low doses of prazepam with extreme caution. If you stop taking it abruptly, you may experience drug-withdrawal symptoms.

Pregnant women should avoid prazepam, since

it could cause birth defects or life-threatening withdrawal symptoms in the newborn child. It should not be used while breast-feeding.

The elderly and children should use small initial doses of prazepam.

Possible Side Effects

Tiredness and drowsiness; inability to concentrate; ataxia; gastric disturbances.

Possible Adverse Effects

Confusion; depression; lethargy; crying; headaches; inactivity; slurred speech; stupor; dizziness; tremors; change in appetite; constipation or diarrhea; dry mouth; nausea; vomiting; inability to control urination; irregular menstrual cycles; changes in heart rhythm; low blood pressure; retention of body fluids; blurred or double vision; itching; rash; hiccups; nervousness; irritability; inability to fall asleep; liver dysfunction.

Prazepam may produce "paradoxical reactions"; while most people are calmed down by use of this drug, a small number become extremely excited, fly into rages, and experience hallucinations and increased anxiety.

Drug Interactions

Prazepam can become extremely dangerous— even deadly—when taken together with alcohol; other tranquilizers; narcotics; anticonvulsants; sleeping pills; barbiturates; and antihistamines.

The effects of prazepam may be stronger when taken together with cimetidine (Tagamet), which is often prescribed to treat ulcers. Prazepam may decrease the effectiveness of the anti-Parkinson drug levodopa.

Heavy smoking may reduce the effectiveness of prazepam. Oral contraceptives may increase its effects.

Usual Dose

20–60 mg. total daily, in divided doses.

Overdose

Mild prazepam overdose causes drowsiness, mental confusion, and lethargy. Serious overdose symptoms include poor muscle coordination; low blood pressure; deep sleep; coma. If you think you are experiencing an overdose, contact your doctor or go to a hospital emergency room immediately. ALWAYS bring the medicine bottle with you.

Generic Name
Protriptyline Hydrochloride

Brand Name

Vivactil

Type of Drug

Tricyclic antidepressant

Prescribed for

Depression

Cautions and Warnings

Do not take protriptyline hydrochloride if you know or suspect you are sensitive or allergic to it or to any other tricyclic drug.

Do not take protriptyline hydrochloride together with alcohol or other depressant drugs.

Because protriptyline hydrochloride may cause drowsiness, use caution while driving, operating potentially dangerous machinery, or performing any task that requires concentration and alertness.

Protriptyline hydrochloride should not be used during the initial period of treatment for a heart attack.

Protriptyline hydrochloride crosses the placental barrier, so it should not be used by pregnant women unless the benefits clearly outweigh the unknown potential hazards to the fetus. It should not be used while breast-feeding.

This drug should be taken with extreme caution if you have a history of convulsive disorders; have trouble urinating; have glaucoma; suffer from heart, liver, or thyroid disease.

Abruptly stopping the use of protriptyline hydrochloride can lead to nausea, headaches, weakness, and an over-all sense of not feeling well. Withdrawal from protriptyline hydrochloride should take place only under a doctor's supervision. While using protriptyline hydrochloride, do not begin or stop taking any other drug (prescription or over-the-counter) without your doctor's approval.

Notify your doctor if extreme dry mouth, difficulty in urinating or excessive sedation occur.

The elderly (those over 60) may become extremely confused during the initial use of protriptyline hydrochloride. They should have regular exams while taking this drug.

Protriptyline hydrochloride should not be used by children.

Possible Side Effects

Drowsiness; dizziness; blurred vision; dry mouth; constipation; difficulty in urinating.

Possible Adverse Effects

Changes in blood pressure; abnormal heart rate; heart attack; stroke; congestive heart failure; confusion (especially in the elderly); hallucinations; disorientation; delusions; anxiety; restlessness; excitement; numbness and tingling in the arms and legs; lack of coordination; muscle spasms or tremors; seizures and/or convulsions; skin rash; itching; ringing in the ears; retention of fluids; fever; stuffy nose; changes in composition of the blood; nausea; vomiting; loss of appetite; stomach upset; diarrhea or constipation; enlargement of the breasts in males and females; increased or decreased sex drive; irregular menstruation; swollen testicles; increased or decreased blood-sugar levels; agitation; insomnia; nightmares; feeling of panic; stomach cramps; black coloration of tongue; yellowing of eyes and/or skin; changes in liver function; weight gain or loss; sweating; flushing; need for frequent urination; drowsiness; dizziness; weakness; headaches; loss of hair.

Drug Interactions

Protriptyline hydrochloride, if taken together with monoamine oxidase (MAO) inhibitors, can lead to a hypertensive crisis, or to high fevers, convulsions, and death. MAO inhibitors should not be used until at least two weeks after the last dose of protriptyline hydrochloride.

Alcohol should be completely avoided while taking protriptyline hydrochloride.

Amphetamines, anticoagulants (blood-thinning drugs), barbiturates and other sedatives, sleeping medications, antihypertension drugs, and thyroid medications should be used with extreme caution while taking protriptyline hydrochloride. If protriptyline hydrochloride is taken together with the sedative Placidyl, delirium may result.

Oral contraceptives may lessen the effects of protriptyline hydrlochloride

Usual Dose

Initial treatment: 15–40 mg. total daily, in divided doses. Lower doses for adolescents and the elderly.

Maintenance treatment: 15–60 mg. total daily, in divided doses. Lower doses for adolescents and the elderly.

Overdose

Symptoms include confusion; inability to concentrate; hallucinations; drowsiness; lowered body temperature; abnormal heart rate; heart failure; enlarged eye pupils; convulsions; dangerously low blood pressure; stupor; agitation; stiffening of muscles; vomiting; high fever; coma; any of the symptoms listed under Possible Adverse Effects. Heart abnormalities caused by an overdose may recur days after other symptoms disappear, even if the overdose was small, so cardiac monitoring is required for at least 72 hours after an overdose. If you think you are experiencing an overdose, contact your doctor or go to a hospital emergency room immediately. ALWAYS bring the medicine bottle with you.

Generic Name
Tranylcypromine Sulfate

Brand Name

Parnate

Type of Drug

Monoamine oxidase (MAO) inhibitor

Prescribed for

Depression

Cautions and Warnings

Tranylcypromine sulfate may cause a hypertensive crisis—i.e., a sudden, potentially deadly increase in blood pressure—when taken with certain foods or other medications. Symptoms of a hypertensive crisis include headache; heart palpitations; stiff or sore neck; nausea; vomiting; excessive sweating; dilated pupils; fear of bright light; irregular heart rhythm; chest pain. If any of these symptoms occur while you are taking tranylcypromine sulfate, contact your doctor or go to a hospital emergency room immediately. ALWAYS bring the medicine bottle with you.

Avoid all foods that may, in combination with MAO inhibitors, increase blood pressure. These include food products that contain tyramine, which is usually (but not always) associated with products that are aged, or that rely on putrefaction to enhance flavor. Specifically, anyone taking tranylcypromine sulfate should not eat or drink the following:

• *Cheeses.* Most cheeses, especially aged ones: blue; Boursault; natural brick; Brie; Camembert; cheddar; Emmentaler; Gruyère; mozzarella; Parmesan; Romano; Roquefort; Stilton.
• *Other dairy products.* Sour cream; yoghurt.
• *Meat/Fish.* Any fish, beef, chicken liver, or other meats allowed to age without refrigeration; any meat prepared with tenderizer; any sausages

(bologna, pepperoni, salami, etc.) containing aged or fermented meats; all game meats; caviar; dried fish, especially salted herring; pickled herring.

• *Alcoholic beverages.* Beer; ale; red wine, especially chianti; sherry; any undistilled beverage. It is wise to avoid *all* alcoholic beverages.

• *Fruits/vegetables/related foods.* Avocadoes; yeast extracts; bananas; canned figs; raisins; soy sauce.

• *Other Foods.* Fava beans; large quantities of chocolate, coffee, tea, colas, and other beverages containing caffeine.

Talk with your doctor before taking any other drug whether prescription or over-the-counter. Also, over-the-counter and prescription hay fever, cold, or weight-reduction drugs should be completely avoided while using tranylcypromine sulfate.

Do not take tranylcypromine sulfate if you know or suspect you are sensitive or allergic to it or to any other MAO inhibitor.

Because tranylcypromine sulfate may cause drowsiness, use caution while driving, operating potentially dangerous machinery, or performing any task that requires concentration and alertness.

The safety of tranylcypromine sulfate during pregnancy has not been established, so it should not be used by pregnant women unless the benefits clearly outweigh the unknown potential hazards to the fetus. It should not be used while breast-feeding

Tranylcypromine sulfate should not be used by adults over 60, or children under 16.

Tranylcypromine sulfate should not be used by anyone with a tumor known as a pheochromocytoma, or by anyone with congestive heart failure; a history of liver disease; kidney problems; cardiovascular disease; a suspected or confirmed problem involving blood supply to the brain; high blood pressure; a history of headaches.

Tranylcypromine sulfate may cause sudden drops in blood pressure when standing up, especially when the drug is first being used. If you suddenly feel dizzy upon standing, lie down until the dizziness passes.

Some tranylcypromine sulfate users experience excessive stimulation, which can usually be controlled by dosage adjustment or briefly stopping the drug under a doctor's supervision.

Tranylcypromine sulfate should be used with caution by epileptics.

Elective surgery requiring general anesthesia, and dental work using anesthesia, should be postponed until several days after the last dose of tranylcypromine sulfate.

Possible Side Effects

Dizziness; weakness; fainting; altered heart rate; vertigo; headaches; overactivity; tremors; muscle twitching; jitteriness; confusion; memory problems; insomnia; fatigue; drowsiness; restlessness; increased anxiety; nausea; diarrhea or constipation; abdominal pain; skin rash or itch; dry mouth; blurry vision; loss of appetite; weight changes; excessive sweating.

Possible Adverse Effects

Euphoria; extreme restlessness; lack of muscle coordination; tenderness; chills; palilalia (repeating words or phrases faster and faster); glaucoma; involuntary eye movements; changes in blood composition; irregular heart rhythm; painful urination; inability to control urine flow; black tongue; sensitivity to light; sexual disturbances. Rare adverse effects include convulsions; hallucinations; acute anxiety; schizophrenia; jaundice; hepatitis; blood-cell destruction; edema; ringing in the ears.

Drug Interactions

Alcoholic beverages containing tyramine should be completely avoided while taking tranylcypromine sulfate. It is wise to avoid *all* alcoholic drinks.

All drugs with stimulant properties should be avoided, including amphetamine; diet drugs; methyldopa; levodopa; dopamine; tryptophan; epinephrine; norepinephrine. Illicit stimulants, including cocaine, should be completely avoided.

Narcotics and other depressant drugs should be used with extreme caution; combining monoamine oxidase (MAO) inhibitors with depressants can lead to convulsions, coma, and death.

Tranylcypromine sulfate should not be used at the same time as any other MAO inhibitor.

Tricyclic antidepressants and related drugs should not be used together with tranylcypromine sulfate. At least 10-14 days should elapse between the last tranylcypromine sulfate dose and the first dose of any other antidepressant or MAO inhibitor.

Local anesthetics should be used cautiously during tranylcypromine sulfate treatment, as should all drugs to treat high blood pressure.

Tranylcypromine sulfate should be used cautiously together with rauwolfia drugs; guanethidine; insulin; oral sulfonylureas. This drug should not be used at the same time as any drug that tends to lower the seizure threshold, such as metrizamide.

Tranylcypromine sulfate should not be used together with anti-Parkinson drugs.

Usual Dose

Initial treatment: 20 mg. total daily, divided into

two doses, gradually increased to 40 mg. total daily, in divided doses.

Maintenance treatment: 10–20 mg. total daily.

Overdose

Symptoms, which may not develop until 12–48 hours after overdose, include excitement; irritability; anxiety; flushing; sweating; irregular heartbeat; irregular muscle movements; exaggerated reflexes; convulsions; altered blood pressure; slowed breathing; coma. If you think you are experiencing an overdose, contact your doctor or go to a hospital emergency room immediately. ALWAYS bring the medicine bottle with you.

Generic Name
Trazodone Hydrochloride

Brand Name

Desyrel

Type of Drug

Antidepressant

Prescribed for

Depression

Cautions and Warnings

Do not take trazodone hydrochloride if you know or suspect you are sensitive or allergic to it.

Alcohol and any drugs that produce a depressant effect should be completely avoided while taking trazodone hydrochloride.

Because trazodone hydrochloride may cause drowsiness, dizziness, blurred vision, or fainting, use caution while driving, operating potentially dangerous machinery, or performing any task that requires concentration and alertness.

The safety of trazodone hydrochloride during pregnancy has not been established, so it should not be used by pregnant women unless the benefits clearly outweigh the unknown potential hazards to the fetus. It should not be used while breast-feeding.

Trazodone hydrochloride should not be used during recovery from a heart attack, and should be used with extreme caution by anyone with heart disease, including arrhythmias.

Electroconvulsive therapy should be avoided while using trazodone hydrochloride.

Males using trazodone hydrochloride may experience prolonged or inappropriate erections; your doctor should be consulted immediately if this occurs, and the drug should be immediately discontinued.

Take trazodone hydrochloride with food.

Children under 18 should not use trazodone hydrochloride.

Possible Side Effects

Drowsiness; dizziness; lightheadedness; fainting; dry mouth; shortness of breath; nausea; vomiting. Notify your doctor if any of these occur.

Possible Adverse Effects

Edema; allergic reactions; rash; skin irritations; numbness; high or low blood pressure; fainting; irregular heartbeat; palpitations; heart attack; mood changes (anger and hostility); nightmares; confusion; decreased concentration; reduced coordination; excitement; fatigue; weakness; headaches; insomnia; impaired memory; nervousness; tremors; hallucinations; mania; impaired speech; delusions; agitation; seizures; ringing in the ears; blurred vision; eye irritation; stuffy nose; changes in sex drive; impotence and other sexual disorders; digestive disturbances; bad taste in mouth; dry mouth; diarrhea or constipation; gas; excess salivation; changes in blood composition; changes in liver; muscle aches; twitches; urinary difficulties; changes in appetite; sweating.

Drug Interactions

Alcohol, barbiturates, sleeping pills, and other drugs that have a depressant effect should be avoided while taking trazodone hydrochloride.

If trazodone hydrochloride is used together with an antihypertensive drug (except clonidine), the dosage of the antihypertensive may have to be reduced.

Monoamine oxidase (MAO) inhibitors should be used with caution with trazodone hydrochloride.

Usual Dose

Initial treatment: 100-150 mg. total daily, gradually increased to maximum 400 mg. total daily.

Maintenance treatment: Smallest effective dose.

Overdose

Most common symptoms are drowsiness and vomiting, although overdose may cause any of the symptoms described in Possible Adverse Effects listed above. If you think you are experiencing an overdose, contact your doctor or go to a hospital emergency room immediately. ALWAYS take the medicine bottle with you.

Brand Name

Triavil

Ingredients

Amitriptyline hydrochloride
(tricyclic antidepressant)
Perphenazine
(phenothiazine antipsychotic)

Type of Drug

Combination

Prescribed for

Depression with anxiety
(This medication contains the same ingredients as Etrafon. For complete information, see p. 113.)

Generic Name
Trimipramine Maleate

Brand Name

Surmontil

Type of Drug

Tricyclic antidepressant

Prescribed for

Depression

Cautions and Warnings

Do not take trimipramine maleate if you know or

suspect you are sensitive or allergic to it or to any other tricyclic drug.

Do not take trimipramine maleate together with alcohol or other depressant drugs.

Because trimipramine maleate may cause drowsiness, use caution while driving, operating potentially dangerous machinery, or performing any task that requires concentration and alertness.

Trimipramine maleate should not be used during the initial period of treatment for a heart attack.

Trimipramine maleate crosses the placental barrier, so it should not be used by pregnant women unless the benefits clearly outweigh the unknown potential hazards to the fetus. It should not be used while breast-feeding.

This drug should be taken with extreme caution if you have a history of convulsive disorders; have trouble urinating; have narrow angle glaucoma; suffer from heart, liver, or thyroid disease.

Abruptly stopping the use of trimipramine maleate can lead to nausea, headaches, weakness, and an over-all sense of not feeling well. Withdrawal from trimipramine maleate should take place only under a doctor's supervision. While using trimipramine maleate, do not begin or stop taking any other drug (prescription or over-the-counter) without your doctor's approval.

Notify your doctor if extreme dry mouth, difficulty in urinating, or excessive sedation occur.

The elderly (those over 60) may become extremely confused during the initial use of trimipramine maleate. They should have regular heart exams while taking this drug.

Trimipramine maleate should not be used by young children.

Possible Side Effects

Drowsiness; dizziness; blurred vision; dry mouth; constipation; difficulty in urinating.

Possible Adverse Effects

Changes in blood pressure; abnormal heart rate; heart attack; stroke; congestive heart failure; confusion (especially in the elderly); hallucinations; disorientation; delusions; anxiety; restlessness; excitement; numbness and tingling in the arms and legs; lack of coordination; muscle spasms or tremors; seizures and/or convulsions; skin rash; itching; ringing in the ears; retention of fluids; fever; stuffy nose; changes in composition of the blood; nausea; vomiting; loss of appetite; stomach upset; diarrhea or constipation; increased or decreased sex drive; irregular menstruation; increased or decreased blood-sugar levels; agitation; insomnia; nightmares; feeling of panic; stomach cramps; black coloration of tongue; yellowing of eyes and/or skin; changes in liver function; weight gain or loss; sweating; flushing; need for frequent urination; drowsiness; dizziness; weakness; headaches; loss of hair.

Drug Interactions

Trimipramine maleate, if taken together with monoamine oxidase (MAO) inhibitors, can lead to a hypertensive crisis, or to high fevers, convulsions, and death. MAO inhibitors should not be used until at least two weeks after the last dose of trimipramine maleate.

Alcohol should be completely avoided while taking trimipramine maleate.

Amphetamines, anticoagulants (blood-thinning drugs), barbiturates and other sedatives, sleeping medications, antihypertension drugs, and thyroid medications should be used with extreme caution while taking trimipramine maleate. If trimipramine maleate is taken together with the sedative Placidyl, delirium may result.

Oral contraceptives may lessen the effects of trimipramine maleate.

Usual Dose

Initial treatment: 75 mg. total daily, in divided doses or single dose at bedtime, increased to maximum 300 mg. total daily. Smaller doses for adolescents and the elderly.

Maintenance treatment: 100–150 mg. total daily in divided doses or single dose at bedtime. Smaller doses for adolescents and the elderly.

Overdose

Symptoms include confusion; inability to concentrate; hallucinations; drowsiness; lowered body temperature; abnormal heart rate; heart failure; enlarged eye pupils; convulsions; dangerously low blood pressure; stupor; agitation; stiffening of muscles; vomiting; high fever; coma; any of the symptoms listed under Possible Adverse Effects. Heart abnormalities caused by an overdose may recur days after other symptoms disappear, even if the overdose was small, so cardiac monitoring is required for at least 72 hours after an overdose. If you think you are experiencing an overdose, contact your doctor or go to a hospital emergency room immediately. ALWAYS bring the medicine bottle with you.

APPENDIX A

PHOBIAS

Your fears may have a proper name. Following is a list of just some of the hundreds of phobias mentioned in medical literature. Some are common, others rare. And all are very real to their victims.

Acrophobia—fear of heights.
Aerophobia—fear of flying.
Agoraphobia—fear of open places.
Ailurophobia—fear of cats.
Algophobia—fear of pain.
Androphobia—fear of men.
Anthophobia—fear of flowers.
Anthropophobia—fear of people.
Apiphobia—fear of bees.
Aquaphobia—fear of water.
Arachnophobia—fear of spiders.
Astraphobia—fear of lightning.
Ballistophobia—fear of bullets or projectiles.
Bathophobia—fear of depth.
Botanophobia—fear of plants.
Brontophobia—fear of thunder.
Chromophobia—fear of certain colors.
Claustrophobia—fear of enclosed places.

Cynophobia—fear of dogs.
Domatophobia—fear of being in a house.
Entomophobia—fear of insects.
Eremophobia—fear of being alone.
Gephyrophobia—fear of bridges.
Gynephobia—fear of women.
Hematophobia—fear of blood.
Iatrophobia—fear of doctors.
Microphobia—fear of germs.
Monophobia—fear of being alone.
Mysophobia—fear of contamination.
Necrophobia—fear of death.
Nosophobia—fear of sickness.
Nyctophobia—fear of darkness.
Ochlophobia—fear of crowds.
Ophidiophobia—fear of snakes.
Ornithophobia—fear of birds.
Panophobia—fear of being afraid.
Pathophobia—fear of disease.
Phonophobia—fear of sounds or speaking aloud.
Psychrophobia—fear of cold.
Pyrophobia—fear of fire.
Sitophobia—fear of food.
Sophophobia—fear of learning.
Syphilophobia—fear of syphilis.
Technophobia—fear of technology.
Thalassophobia—fear of the ocean.
Thanatophobia—fear of imminent death.
Topophobia—fear of particular locales.
Trichophobia—fear of hair.
Verbophobia—fear of words.
Xenophobia—fear of strangers.
Zoophobia—fear of animals.

APPENDIX B

SOME PHYSICAL ILLNESSES THAT CAN CAUSE ANXIETY

Cardiovascular:	Angina pectoris
	Congestive heart disease
	Hypertension
	Heart attack
	Arrhythmia
	Mitral valve prolapse
	Vascular diseases
	Syncope
	Hypovolemia
Respiratory:	Asthma
	Pneumonia
	Pneumothorax
	Pulmonary embolism
	Pulmonary edema
	Chronic obstructive pulmonary disease
Neurologic:	Migraine headache
	Postconcussion syndrome
	Seizure disorder—temporal lobe

Organic brain syndrome
Intracranial mass lesion
Encephalopathies (toxic,
  metabolic, infectious)
Essential tremor
Vertigo
Multiple sclerosis

Metabolic/endocrine:	Hyperthyroidism/hypothyroidism
	Hypoglycemia
	Menopause
	Cushing's disease
	Hyperthermia
	Hypoparathyroidism
	Porphyria
	Hyperkalemia
	Hypocalcemia
Neoplastic:	Hormone-secreting tumors (carcinoid, insulinoma, pheochromocytoma)
	Cerebral neoplasm
Hematologic:	Anemias
Immunologic:	Anaphylaxis
	Lupus erythematosus
Infections:	Viral hepatitis
	Infectious mononucleosis
	Brucella

APPENDIX C

SOME DRUGS THAT CAN CAUSE ANXIETY

Type of Drug	Generic Names	Brand Names
CARDIOVASCULAR	digitalis	[overdosage can result in anxiety]
	digitoxin	Crystodigin Purodigin
	timolol maleate	Blocadren
STIMULANTS	dextroamphetamine sulfate	Dexampex Dexedrine Ferndex Oxydess II Spancap Tidex
	amphetamines	(all)
	methamphetamine hydrochloride	Desoxyn Methampex
	methylphenidate hydrochloride	Ritalin
	phenmetrazine	Preludin

Type of Drug	Generic Names	Brand Names
	caffeine	Vivarin No Doz Tirend Caffedrine Quick Pep
	cocaine	
CHOLINERGIC BLOCKERS	atropine scopolamine	
PARASYMPATHOLYTICS	(all)	[overdosage can result in anxiety]
ORAL AND NOSE AGENTS	ephedrine	Efedron Vatronol
	pseudoephedrine	Cenafed Halofed Sudrin Neofed Sudafed
ANTIPARKINSON AGENTS	levodopa	Dopar Lardopa
SPASMOLYTICS	aminophylline	Aminodur Dura-Tabs Aminophyllin Somophyllin Lixaminol Phyllocontin
ARTHRITIS DRUG	indomethacin	Indocin
ANTIPSYCHOTICS	(all)	[may produce a condition marked by motor restlessness]
OTHER DRUGS AND FOODS	alcohol monosodium glutamate	

APPENDIX D

SOME PHYSICAL ILLNESSES THAT CAN CAUSE DEPRESSION

Neurologic	Epilepsy
	Parkinson's disease
	Multiple sclerosis
	Postconcussion syndrome
	Narcolepsy
	Partial complex seizures
	Normal pressure hydrocephalus
	Huntington's chorea
	Pick's disease
	Tumors
Infections	Viral hepatitis
	Infectious mononucleosis
	Tuberculosis
	Viral pneumonia
	Brucella
	Syphilis
	Viral and bacterial infections
Metabolic/ endocrine	Hyper-/hypothyroidism
	Diabetes mellitus

	Hypoglycemia
	Cushing's disease
	Addison's disease
	Hyperparathyroidism
	Pheochromocytoma
	Cancer
	Ovarian failure
	Testicular failure
	Hypo-/hypercalcemia
	Panhypopituitarism
	Wilson's disease
	Porphyria
Hematologic	Anemia
	Blood abnormalities
Cardiovascular	Arteriosclerosis
	Stroke
	Congestive heart failure
	Mitral valve prolapse
	Arterial embolism
Immunologic	Lupus
Others	Organic brain syndrome
	Arthritis
	Vitamin deficiencies
	Toxins and heavy metals
	Drug abuse
	Drug withdrawal
	Various degenerative diseases

APPENDIX E

SOME DRUGS THAT CAN CAUSE DEPRESSION

Type of Drug	Generic Names	Brand Names
AMEBECIDES and TRICHOMONACIDES [drug of choice for amoebic dysentery and trichomonal infections]	metronidazole	Flagyl Metryl Protostat Satric

SULFONAMIDES [drugs of choice for urinary tract infections, conjunctivitis, toxoplasmosis, and trachoma]	co-trimoxazole
	sulfamethoxa-
	  zole
	  and trimetho-
	  prim]
		Bactrim
		Septra
		Cotrim
		Bethaprim

	sulfacytine	Renoquid
	sulfadiazine	Microsulfon
	sulfamethizole	Proklar Thiosulfil
	sulfamethoxa- zole	Gantanol Gamazole Urobak
	sulfapyridine	Sulfapyridine
	sulfasalazine	Azulfidine

Type of Drug	Generic Names	Brand Names
		Azaline
		Azulfidine-EN-tabs
		S.A.S.-500
	sulfisoxazole	Gantrisin
		SK-Soxazole
ANTI-INFECTIVES [provide broad protection against several infectious diseases]	amantadine hydrochloride [also used to treat Parkinson's disease]	Symmetrel
	chlorampheni	Chloromycetin Kapseals
		Mychel
CARDIOVASCULAR SYSTEM DRUGS antiarrhythmics	disopyramide phosphate	Norpace
	procainamide hydrochloride	Procan SR Promine
		Pronestyl
		Sub-Quin
beta blockers antihypertensives [used in treatment of high blood pressure]	(all) alseroxylon	Rauwiloid
	deserpidine	Harmonyl
	methyldopa	Aldomet
	guanabenz acetate	Wytensin
	clonidine hydrochloride	Catapres
	guanethidine sulfate	Ismelin

Type of Drug	Generic Names	Brand Names
	guanadrel sulfate	Hylorel
	hydralazine hydrochloride	Apresoline Alazine
	metyrosine	Demser
	prazosin hydrochloride	Minipress
	rauwolfia derivatives	Hiwolfia Raudixin Rauval Rauverid Rauwolfia Rawfola Rauserpin Wolfina Serfolia
	rescinnamine	Moderil
	reserpine	Releserp-5 Reserpoid Sandril Serpalan Serpasil Serpate SK-Reserpine Zepine
MORPHINELIKE ANALGESICS [relief of moderate to severe pain]	nalbuphine hydrochloride	Nubain
CENTRAL NERVOUS SYSTEM DRUGS nonsteroidal anti-inflammatory agents	indomethacin	Indocin Indocin SR
	fenoprofen	Nalfon

Type of Drug	Generic Names	Brand Names
arthritis drugs	ibuprofen	Advil Motrin
	naproxen	Anaprox Naprosyn
	sulindac	Clinoril
anticonvulsants [used to treat seizure disorders]	mephenytoin	Mesantoin
	methsuximide	Celontin Kapseals
	phenacemide	Phenurone
	valproic acid	Depakene Depakote
	clonazepam	Clonopin
tranquilizers [used to treat anxiety and tension]	chlormezanone	Trancopal Caplets
cerebral stimulants [used to treat obesity]	fenfluramine hydrochloride	Pondimin
	mazindol	Mazanor Sanorex
	pemoline	Cylert
AUTONOMIC NERVOUS SYSTEM DRUG cholinergic blocker [used to treat Parkinsonism and dyskinesia]	benztropine mesylate	Congentin
GASTROINTESTINAL TRACT	apomorphine hydrochloride	Apomorphine
HORMONAL AGENTS fibrocystic breast disease	danazol	Danocrine
contraceptive	estrogen with progestins	Enovid Norinyl

Type of Drug	Generic Names	Brand Names
		Ortho-Novum
estrogens	chlorotrianisene	Tace
	diethylstil-bestrol	Diethylstilbestrol
	estrified estrogens	Estratab Evex Menest
	estradiol	Estrace
	conjugated estrogens	Premarin Evestrone
	ethinyl estradiol	Estinyl Feminone
	quinestrol	Estrovis
progestins	medroxypro-gesterone acetate	Amen Curretab Provera
	norethindrone	Norlutin
	norethindrone acetate	Norlutate
contraceptives	norgestrel	Ovrette
antineoplastic agents	procarbazine hydrochloride	Matulane
	mitotane	Lysodren
	vinblastine sulfate	Velban
miscellaneous drugs	clomiphene citrate	Clomid Serophene
	levodopa	Dopar Larodopa Sinemet
	carbidopa	Lodosyn

SOURCES

Adler, Jerry, *et al.* "The Fight to Conquer Fear." *Newsweek,* 23 April 1984.

Alexander, Tom. "The New Technology of the Mind." *Fortune,* 24 January 1983.

Barley, Betsy. "Coping with Travel Phobias." *Travel & Leisure,* August, 1984.

Begley, Sharon. "The SAD Days of Winter." *Newsweek,* 14 January 1985.

Berger, Stuart. "Food Can Change Your Mood." *Parade Magazine,* 23 December 1984.

"Biochemical Markers Identify Mental States." *Science,* 2 October 1981.

Boffey, Philip M. "The 'Holiday Blues' Are Overstated, Health Experts Find." *New York Times,* 24 December 1983.

Boyd, J.R., ed. *Facts and Comparisons.* St. Louis: J.B. Lippincott, 1984.

Brody, Jane. *Jane Brody's The New York Times Guide to Personal Health.* New York: Times Books, 1982.

——. "Personal Health: Helping Parents to Cope with Tragedy, the Death of a Child." *New York Times,* 16 February 1983.

——. "Personal Health. Panic Attacks: The Terror is Treatable." *New York Times*, 19 October 1983.

——. "Surprising Health Impact Discovered for Light." *New York Times,* 13 November 1984.

"Can Depression Be Categorized?" *Journal of the American Medical Association* 18, April 1980.

Carey, John, and Mary Bruno. "Why Cynicism Can Be Fatal." *Newsweek*, 10 September 1984.

"Chance of Depression Relapse Is Found to Wane with Time." *New York Times*, 8 January 1984.

"Childhood Depression: New—and Old—Ways to Spot It." *Medical World News*, 1 March 1982.

Chilnick, Lawrence D., ed. *The Little Black Pill Book.* New York: Bantam Books, 1983.

The Pill Book. 2d ed. New York: Bantam Books, 1982.

"Classes on Coping." *Wall Street Journal*, 17 August 1984.

"Clinical Trial of Psychotherapies Is Under Way." *Science,* April 1981.

"Coping with Grief—It Can't Be Rushed." *U.S. News & World Report*, 14 November 1983.

"Depression." *Health Facts,* Centers for Medical Consumers and Health Care Information, Inc., Jan/ Feb 1978.

"Depression? Vielleicht Leigt's an der Schilddruse?" *Wiesbaden* (Germany) *Medical Tribune,* 31 August 1981.

"DST May Be Marker for Major Depressive Disorder in Adolescents." *Clinical Psychiatry News*, June 1982.

"DST: Pinpointing Depression." *Sciences News*, 23 May 1981.

Eckholm, Erik. "Value of Medication Against Stress Now Questioned." *New York Times*, 24 July 1984.

"ECT: Shocking Depression." *Science News*, 23 May 1981.

"Fair Oaks Group Presents Papers at the 135th Annual A.P.A. Association Meeting" *New Jersey Psychiatric Association Newsletter*, June 1982.

"A Genetic Thread May Bind Depressed Families." *New Scientist*, 17 December 1918.

Gold, Mark S., *et al.* "The Psychiatric Laboratory." *Clinical Psychopharmacology.* John Wright PSG, Inc., 1984.

——"Substance Induced Organic Mental Disorders." *American Psychiatric Press; Psychiatry Update*, vol. 4, ch. 12, forthcoming.

"Hormone Is Marker in Bipolar Disorders." *American Psychiatric Association News Bulletin*, 3–9 May 1980.

How Long Do Depressions Last? Depression Notes. Lakeside Laboratories (Wisconsin) pamphlet, 1974.

Kovaks, Maria, *et al.* "Depressed Outpatients Treated with Cognitive Therapy or Pharmacotherapy." *Archives of General Psychiatry*, January 1981.

Lechky, Olga. "Psychiatrists Now Have Test to Help Sort Out Depressions." (Toronto) *Medical Post*, 20 October 1981.

Leo, John. "Learning to Love With the Blues." *Time*, 18 June 1984.

——."Polling for Mental Health." *Time*, 15 October 1984.

——. "The Ups and Downs of Creativity." *Time*, 8 October 1984.

"The Machinery of Depression." *Science News*, 9 August 1980.

Machlowitz, Marilyn. "New Theories of Depression Hold Promise of Simpler Remedy." *New York Times*, 6 February 1981.

"Of Grief and Morbidity: Can Stress and Grief Depress Immunity?" *Journal of the American Medical Association*, 23/30 July 1982.

"Patients Appearing Depressed May Have SAT, Says Researcher." *Psychiatric News*, 3 September 1982.

Physicians' Desk Reference. 39th ed. Oradell, New Jersey: Medical Economics Company, 1984.

Price, John Scott. "Chronic Depressive Illness." *British Medical Journal*, 6 May 1978.

Rosanbaum, Jerrold F. "The Drug Treatment of Anxiety." *New England Journal of Medicine*, 18 February 1982.

Rounsaville, Bruce J., *et al.* "Do Psychotherapy and Pharmacotherapy for Depression Conflict?" *Archives of General Psychiatry*, January 1981.

Rovner, Sandy. "Shedding Light on Moods." *Washington Post*, 24 June 1983.

Schatzberg, Alan F., *et al.* "Platelet Monoamine Oxidase and Dexamethasone Suppression Test Results in Depressed Patients." Papers on New Research in Summary Form, 136th Annual Meeting of the American Psychiatric Association, 30 April–6 May 1983.

Snider, Arthur J. *A Doctor Discusses Learning How to Live with Nervous Tension.* Budlong Press Co., Chicago, Ill. 1980.

"Social Causes of Depression." *The Lancet*, 24 June 1978.

Sullivan, Walter. "Genetic Maker May Reveal Manic-Depressive Disorder." *New York Times*, 26 July 1984.

——. "Scientists Study Brain's 'Teamwork.'" *New York Times*, 10 October 1984.

Thornton, Jeannye. "Behind a Surge in Suicides of Young People." *U.S. News & World Report*, 20 June 1983.

Trafford, Abigail. "New Hope for the Depressed." *U.S. News & World Report*, 24 January 1983.

——. "Doctors Gain Understanding of Depression, Improving Chances of Effective Treatment." *Wall Street Journal*, 5 May 1982.

West, Eric D. "Electric Convulsion Therapy in Depression: A Double-Blind Controlled Trial." *British Medical Journal*, 31 January 1981.

Whitlow, Joan. "Drugs Helping Control Major Panic Disorders." (Newark) *Star-Ledger*, 5 December 1982.

——. "Fair Oaks Research Team Links Addiction, Depression." (Newark) *Sunday Star-Ledger*, 8 May 1983.

"Why 30,000 Americans Will Commit Suicide This Year." *U.S. News & World Report*, 2 April 1984.

Widmer, Reuben B. "Early Identification of the Depressed Patient." Family Practice Recertification. January 1982.

"Widows Form Group." *Senior News*, June 1984.

INDEX

Index of Generic and Brand Name Drugs

Note: Generic names are printed in **boldface** type.

Adapin, 110–13, plate A
Alprozalam, 32, 72, 80–82
Amitril, 83–86
Amitriptyline hydrochloride, 74, 83–86, plate A
See also Etrafon; Limbitrol; Triavil
Amobarbital, 72, 86–88
Amobarbital sodium, 72, 89–91
Amoxapine, 71, 91–94
Amytal, 86–88, plate A
Amytal Sodium Pulvules, 89–91
Anxanil, 120–21
A-Poxide, 96–99
Asendin, 91–94, plate A
Atarax, 120–21, plate A

Ativan, 137–40, plate A
Atozine, 120–21
Aventyl Hydrochloride, 150–53

Benactyzine hydrochloride, *see* Deprol
Bupropion, 76–77, 94–96
Buspirone, 33

Centrax, 161–63, plate A
Chlordiazepoxide, *see* Limbitrol
Chlordiazepoxide hydrochloride, 72, 96–99
Chlorpromazine hydrochloride, 79

Clorazepate dipotassium, 72, 99–101

Dalmane, 32
Deprol, 78, 101–3
Desipramine hydrochloride, 74, 104–7
Desyrel, 171–73, plate A
Diazepam, 72, 107–9
Doxepin hydrochloride, 74, 110–13
Durrax, 120–21

Elavil, 83–86, plates A and B
Emitrip, 83–86
Endep, 83–86, plate B
Equanil, 145–48, plate B
Equanil Tablets and Wyseals, 145–48
Eskalith, 133–37, plate B
Etrafon, 78, 113–17, plate B

Halazepam, 72, 117–20
Hydroxyzine hydrochloride, 74, 120–21
Hydroxyzine pamoate, 74, 120–21
Hy-Pam, 120–21

Imipramine, 32, 74, 122–25
Imipramine hydrochloride, 74, 122–25

Imipramine pamoate, 74, 122–25
Inderal, 79
Isocarboxazid, 76, 125–29

Janimine, 122–25

Libritabs, 96–99
Librium, 32, 96–99, plate B
Limbitrol, 78, 129–33, plate B
Lipoxide, 96–99
Lithane, 133–37
Lithium, 67, 68, 77–78, 133–37
Lithium Carbonate, 133–37
Lithobid, 133–37
Lithonate, 133–37
Lithotabs, 133–37
Lorazepam, 73, 137–40
Ludiomil, 140–43, plate C

Maprotiline hydrochloride, 74, 140–43
Marplan, 125–29
Mebaral, 143–45
Mephobarbital, 72, 143–45
Mepriam, 145–48
Meprobamate, 32, 74, 145–48
See also Deprol
Meprospan, 145–48, plate C
Merital, 148–50, plate C

Miltown, 145–48, plate C
Murcil, 96–99

Nardil, 156–60, plate C
Neuramate, 145–48
Neurate-400, 145–48
Nomifensine maleate,
67–68, 76, 77,
148–50
Norpramin, 104–7, plate C
**Nortriptyline hydrochlo-
ride,** 74, 150–53

Oxazepam, 73, 154–56

Pamelor, 150–53
Parnate, 166–71, plate C
Paxipam, 117–20
Perphenazine, *see* Etrafon;
Limbitrol
Pertofrane, 104–7
Phenelzine, 32
Phenelzine sulfate, 76,
156–60
Prazepam, 73, 161–63
Propranolol, 79
Protriptyline hydrochloride,
74, 163–66

Reposans-10, 96–99

Sedabamate, 145–48
Serax, 154–56

Sereen, 96–99
Sinequan, 110–13, plate C
SK-Amitriptyline, 83–86
SK-Bamate, 145–48
SK-Lygen, 96–99, plate C
SK-Pramine, 122–25, plate
C
Surmontil, 174–77, plate C

**Thioridazine hydrochlo-
ride,** 79
Tipramine, 122–25
Tofranil, 122–25, plate C
Tranmep, 145–48
Tranxene, 99–101, plate D
Tranylcypromine sulfate,
76, 166–71
Trazodone hydrochloride,
67–68, 76, 77, 171–73
Triavil, 78, 113–17, plate D
Trifluoperazine, 79
Trimipramine maleate, 75,
174–77

Valium, 32, 107–9, plate
D
Valrelease, 107–9
Vamate, 120–21
Vistaril, 120–21, plate D
Vivactil, 163–66, plate D

Wellbutrin, 94–96

Xanax, 80–82, plate D

ABOUT THE MEDICAL CONSULTANT

ALAN F. SCHATZBERG, M.D., is Associate Professor of Psychiatry and currently Interim Psychiatrist-in-Chief at McLean Hospital, a teaching hospital of Harvard Medical School, in Belmont, Massachusetts. Dr. Schatzberg is a well-known psychiatric researcher in the biology and pharmacological treatment of depression and is the author of over 100 medical reports on depression and anxiety. He is a Fellow of the American Psychiatric Association and is certified by the American Board of Psychiatry and Neurology. He is also a member of both the American College of Psychiatrists and the American College of Neuropsychopharmacology.

Dr. Schatzberg is a graduate of New York University School of Medicine. He did his psychiatric residency at the Massachusetts Mental Health Center and was also a Clinical Fellow in Psychiatry at Harvard Medical School. After two years of military service, he joined the staff of McLean Hospital where prior to his current position he served as the Chief of Specialty Services and Co-Director of the Affective Disease Program. He and his wife and two children live in the Boston area.

BANTAM'S PILL BOOK LIBRARY

— ℞ —